# Getting Ahead

A SWEDISH IMMIGRANT'S
REMINISCENCES, 1834–1887

By Charles J. Hoflund

Edited by H. Arnold Barton

SOUTHERN ILLINOIS UNIVERSITY PRESS

CARBONDALE AND EDWARDSVILLE

Copyright © 1989 by the Board of Trustees,
Southern Illinois University
All rights reserved
Printed in the United States of America
Designed by Joanna Hill Design
Production supervised by Natalia Nadraga
92  91  90  89    4  3  2  1

Library of Congress Cataloging-in-Publication Data

Hoflund, Charles J. (Charles John), 1834–1914.
Getting ahead: a Swedish immigrant's reminiscences, 1834–1887 / by
Charles J. Hoflund; edited by H. Arnold Barton.
p.  cm.
Bibliography: p.
Includes index.
ISBN 0-8093-1521-1
1. Hoflund, Charles J. (Charles John), 1834–1914.  2. Swedish
Americans – Biography.  3. Immigrants – United States – Biography.
4. United States – Emigration and immigration – History – 19th century.
5. Sweden – Emigration and immigration – History – 19th century.
I. Barton, H. Arnold (Hildor Arnold), 1929– .    II. Title.
E184.S23H564 1989
973'.04397 – dc19                                          88-30299
                                                              CIP

The paper used in this publication meets the minimum requirements of
American National Standard for Information Sciences – Permanence
of Paper for Printed Library Materials, ANSI Z39.48-1984. ⊗

# Contents

# Illustrations

(after page 41)

# Introduction

Carl Johan Hoflund was born in Sweden in 1834 and emigrated to the United States in 1850, at the age of sixteen, after which he called himself Charles J. Hoflund. At the end of his life, in 1913, he dictated his reminiscences to his eighteen-year-old grandson, Stanley Hoflund High, who typed them out under the title, "The Autobiography of Charles John Hoflund."

Fifty-eight years later, a grand-nephew, David Lauren Hoffland of San Diego, privately published his *Hoflund: The History of a Swedish-American Family from 1655 to 1970,* in 1971, which included portions of Charles Hoflund's autobiography.[1] At the same time, he made available an excerpt from the autobiography, covering the Hoflund family's journey to America in 1850 (pages 23 to 24 in this book), to Professor Franklin D. Scott, then editor of the *Swedish Pioneer Historical Quarterly,* which came out in that journal the same year.[2]

Another decade and a half went by. Then, in 1986, a friend in Djursdala, Charles Hoflund's native parish in Sweden, sent me a Swedish translation of the complete autobiography. This had been made by Bertil Karlsson, a teacher in nearby Vimmerby distantly related to the Hoflund family, and had just been published locally.[3] While visiting Hoflund relatives in Rockford, Illinois, Karlsson had learned of the autobiography and obtained a copy. Through him, I was then able to contact these same Hoflund descendants and myself acquire a copy of the entire manuscript in English.

The story of this manuscript, from its composition in 1913 to its publication for a wider interested public over three-quarters of a century later, is a notable example and reminder of that great hidden wealth of personal reminiscences conceived and venerated as purely family "heirlooms," despite all they can contribute to our broader understanding of the past. "History," as Thomas Carlyle reminds us, "is the essence of innumerable biographies."

Charles Hoflund provides a fresh and engaging picture of the times and places he experienced. He was an active participant in the events described, and although he was a man of little schooling, he was an intelligent, well-informed, and articulate observer, blessed with a keen memory. His life reflected, moreover, many of the broader characteristics and currents of his era.

Many Americans by choice have recorded their reminiscences, but Hoflund's are exceptional in the balanced treatment they give to life in both the old country and the new, since so many tend to neglect either the one or the other. The result is a remarkably well-integrated account, despite the geographical and cultural distances separating the places in which Hoflund lived his life.

It is worth noting the special value of early emigrants' recorded recollections of their home localities in the lands of their origins. Even where literacy was widespread at the time the great migration began, as it was in Sweden, those who remained at home rarely wrote about how things were during their younger years. Or if they did, their memories could have been gradually and imperceptibly affected by later developments. Thus Charles Hoflund's childhood recollections (translated by Bertil Karlsson) are now considered in Djursdala and the surrounding area a uniquely valuable source regarding local life around the middle of the nineteenth century.

The experiences of Charles Hoflund and his family make a good story in themselves. But they gain a greater historic significance for being highly typical representatives of the Swedish emigrants in general at the beginning of their great migration to America. Although scattered individuals had come from Sweden earlier, the Swedish migration is traditionally considered to have begun with Gustaf Unonius, whose departure in 1841 aroused considerable attention and whose published letters from Wisconsin were widely read and discussed. The first group of Swedish peasants to travel and settle together in America was led by Peter Cassel from southern Östergötland province to southeastern Iowa in 1845. During the years immediately following, the parishes along the provincial boundary between Östergötland and Småland — including Djursala, the Hoflunds' home parish — contributed a large part of the earliest Swedish emigration.[4]

The Hoflunds were likewise representative of the early emigrants in terms of their social and economic status. Characteristically they were a family of some means and standing. Peter Cassel wrote back to Sweden in 1846 that a family of four should not consider coming to America with less than one thousand *riksdaler*.[5] This was a fairly considerable sum at that time, and the Hoflund family consisted of eight persons. To be sure, they were hard pressed upon arriving in Illinois, but for them all to make the journey together was no small accomplishment economically. It was nonetheless typical of their period that the emigrants came over as complete families, rather than as individuals, often in the company of larger groups on their way to localities where relatives and friends from home were already settled. Emigration from the poorer classes would not begin on a large scale until the 1880s, when immigrants well established in American could send money or prepaid tickets home to the Old Country.

Charles Hoflund was not much given to analyzing or explaining motives, but it is clear from his family's relatively favorable circumstances in Sweden and what he tells of his own pessimistic reflections over his future if he were to remain there that—again characteristically for the earlier Swedish emigration—his family left not because of actual poverty but because of the fear of eventual impoverishment and the social degradation it would bring. At the same time, the powerful impressions produced by the "America-letters" sent home by even earlier emigrants, as Hoflund describes them, reveal how the passive and fatalistic attitudes of an ancient and traditional peasant society were beginning to give way to new ideas of improvement through individual will and effort. Families like the Hoflunds, who were well enough situated in life to be able to envision even greater possibilities, were those most likely to harken to such a message and face a new destiny beyond the sea. Typically their bold undertaking aroused deep misgivings among their more traditionally minded neighbors.

The family was typical, too, in its choice of destination, to which earlier emigrants from home had found their way over the past few years. Already in 1846, the year after Peter Cassel had established his New Sweden colony in neighboring southeastern Iowa, Henry County and its immediate environs in northwestern Illinois had become the main focus of Swedish immigration, and remained so down to the Civil War. Here the family made its home. In coming from Djursdala in Småland to Andover, Illinois, in 1850, the Hoflunds—like most of their countrymen who emigrated in this early period – moved directly from one of the still most archaic and tradition-bound regions of their homeland to the advancing frontier in the American prairie Midwest, with its rough-and-ready yet rapidly evolving new society.

Still, bewildering as such a drastic cultural contrast might be, Charles Hoflund, like most of his fellow immigrants both then and later, had little time or opportunity to reflect very deeply upon it at the time, which was probably a somewhat disguised blessing in easing their transition. Already the day after the family's arrival at Andover, Charles was hired to work for a nearby Yankee farmer, allowing him to earn his own keep and contribute to his family's depleted assets. Characteristically for the earlier Swedish immigrants, both Charles and others in his family would prove remarkably mobile and adaptable, with regard both to kinds and places of work, as they determinedly forged their way ahead by seizing whatever opportunities came their way. Like so many of his generation of immigrants, Charles Hoflund was proud of the breadth and variety of the experiences life brought him and avid to make good the deficiencies of his schooling by educating himself to become an informed citizen of his adopted homeland and the world he lived in.

Finally, he was typical of the early Swedish immigrants of peasant background in apparently experiencing no real crisis of identity in the new land. He arrived in America at a time when less than four thousand of his countrymen were to be found there. Those who came over during the 1840s and 1850s were fully prepared and indeed eager to adapt as quickly as possible to American ways and speech, having no intention and usually no possibility of returning, and seeing no real prospects for preserving their customs or language in the long run. The concept of a "Swedish-America," which should preserve the heritage of the Old Country for the benefit both of the immigrants themselves and of America's evolving national culture, did not actually begin to emerge before the 1880s, following the far heavier emigration that from the later 1860s on vastly increased the critical mass of the Swedish element in the United States. It was then that the perplexing question of what it meant to be a "Swedish-American" became the subject of considerable soul-searching.[6] While always proud of his origins and generally most comfortable living in areas of Swedish settlement, Charles Hoflund considered himself, simply and naturally, an American among Americans.

Despite the title of the manuscript, Charles Hoflund's account of his life does not comprise his complete autobiography. It is most detailed up to 1860, the year of his marriage, and it ends in 1887, the year he moved from Illinois to Nebraska, when he was fifty-three years old and still had twenty-seven years to live. Perhaps we may be grateful that this was so, considering the many autobiographical accounts that lose their color and vivacity as they settle into the routine and complacency of their authors' later years. By 1887, Charles Hoflund had made it in life. His years of striving and adventure were past.

After that, there is not so much that need be added. He was the proprietor of a bank in Beemer, Nebraska, assisted by his sons Charles E. and Oliver Hoflund, from 1887 until 1891. He then sold his interest and moved to Chicago, where he traded on the grain exchange, well turned-out, it is recalled, in top hat and tails. In 1895 he retired altogether from business life. Thereafter he lived first with his son Charles in Sioux City, Iowa, then in Omaha, Nebraska, until his death at the age of eighty in 1914. His wife, Christine, followed him in death in 1928. Both are buried, together with other members of the Hoflund family, in the Methodist cemetery in Andover, Illinois.

For Charles Hoflund, the reminiscences he dictated in 1913 were the summation of a long and varied life. For young Stanley Hoflund High, who transcribed them, this collaboration was the beginning of a successful career of editing and writing. After graduating from college and serving as a pilot in World War I, he went on to become editor of the *Christian Herald*, a foreign-affairs commentator for the National Broadcasting Corporation, a speech writer for Herbert Hoover, Franklin D. Roosevelt, Thomas E. Dewey, and Dwight D. Eisenhower, and a senior editor of the *Reader's Digest*.[7]

Charles Hoflund's life story holds a particular fascination for me, since my own earliest forebears from Sweden to come to America arrived in the Midwest around the same time. But there is another, more personal reason. Hoflund relates that his family sat on Sundays in the "third or fourth pew" in Djursdala church. During those very years, my own paternal great-grandfather's family sat in the third pew of the same church, until they too followed earlier relatives across the ocean in 1867, as I have recounted elsewhere.[8] I know Djursdala well. Strong bonds of affection attach me to that place and to my many relatives and friends there and nearby.

In preparing Charles Hoflund and Stanley High's manuscript for publication, I have sought to leave it as much as possible in its original form. My editorial changes are therefore minimal. I have divided it into chapters, for which I have provided titles. In places, I have broken down excessively long paragraphs into shorter ones. Where called for, I have corrected the spelling of place names, particularly in Sweden, and of Swedish words, since Stanley High was apparently little familiar with the Swedish language, or at least its orthography. A few unnecessary Swedish words, following their English equivalents in parentheses, have been eliminated, while obviously missing or in some cases clarifying words have been inserted in square brackets. Some changes or additions to the punctuation have been made in the interests of clarity. A copy of the original manuscript is now deposited at the Swenson Swedish Immigration Research Center at Augustana College, Rock Island, Illinois.

Finally, let me acknowledge my gratitude to several persons who have helped me in bringing out these valuable reminiscences. Gösta Karlsson of Djursdala sent me the Swedish translation of the manuscript in 1986, and its translator, Bertil Karlsson of Vimmerby, helped me to locate the Hoflund descendants in America. The first of these I contacted, Violet Hofflund of Rockford, Illinois, gave both useful information and encouragement, putting me in touch with her sister Anna and late brother-in-law Ernest H. Jackson, also of Rockford, who provided me with a copy of the manuscript. Charles Hoflund's granddaughters, Winifred Harvey of Adelphi, Maryland, Ruth Warrick of Meadow Grove, Nebraska, and Grace Gregg of Hawarden, Iowa, have graciously permitted this publication of their grandfather's reminiscences. Mrs. Gregg and Miss Hofflund provided family photographs. I received valuable help in assembling other pictorial material from Ronald E. Nelson of the Bishop Hill Heritage Association, Bishop Hill Illinois; Mary Michaels and Gary T. Stockton of the Illinois State Historical Library, Springfield; Doris Wherry-Maxwell of the Western District Library, Orion, Illinois; and Åsa Torbeck of Nordiska Museet, Stockholm.

I am grateful to Angela K. Calcaterra for typing material I myself have written for this book, and to Stephen W. Smith for copy editing the manuscript. And, as always, I am thankful for the help, encouragement, and patience of my wife, Aina Margareta.

H.A.B.

Carbondale, Illinois

# Getting Ahead

# Preface

As long as I can remember the stories of Grandpa Hoflund's early experiences have had a fascination for me. And ever since I first heard the idea of having a written account of them I have been deeply interested in preparing this book. I recall the numerous letters I wrote to Grandpa urging him to keep at his task, and every Christmas when the Hoflunds gathered to enjoy the Holidays everyone was anxious to know of the progress made. But when we moved to Omaha in 1913 I found the greater part of the work was still ahead and to write it by hand seemed an almost endless undertaking. After talking with my Uncle Charles, we hired a typewriter and started to work.

Grandpa would sit in his big easy chair near the window and dictate to me by the hour. It seemed to afford him a great deal of pleasure and whenever forced to lay aside the work for a time he would grow anxious and insist on continuing. The book is exactly as he dictated it to me. His grammar and sentence construction were remarkably perfect, while his memory of the smallest details in each incident was wonderful. When the work was finally completed Grandpa seemed lost, for he had been entirely wrapped up in the book and but for school it would have been a pleasure to have carried the story up to date although the incidents of his life in recent years have not been unusual or especially interesting.

I feel proud to have been permitted to help in the completion of this book. Grandpa Hoflund had a great mind and a strength of character very seldom surpassed. He was unusually well read and conversant upon all subjects. With the opportunities of youth today, I am sure Grandpa Hoflund would have occupied a high place in the nation's life.

1913                                     STANLEY HOFLUND HIGH

# I

# The Old Country,

## 1834–1850

For years I have contemplated writing a short and simple narrative of the most important events of my life. But at this late date (I am now in my seventieth year), it can not be expected that I will be able to do but slight justice to a theme that, in the hands of a more competent narrator, might be very interesting. I have had no preparation for work of this kind and very likely I would not have undertaken the task had it not been for the urgent request of my children, and especially Oliver, my youngest son.

I was born in Djursdala, Kalmar *län*, Sweden, October 11th, 1834.[1] My parents were Gustaf Peter Hoflund and Anna Brita Hoflund (née Carlsdotter). My father and also my grandfather were born in the same place.

My grandfather's name was Nicolas Hoflund; he lived to be eighty years old and of him I have a very vivid recollection. He was a little lame, but must have been a very strong man, rather below medium height, but very heavy-set. As I remember him, he had a pleasing personality, and I was always glad when he came to our house, as he did quite often. Then Father would shave him, give him something to eat and a drink of homemade whiskey (as was the custom), and Grandfather would often say, "Oh, Gustaf, you do too much for me." I was about thirteen years old when Grandfather Hoflund died.[2]

Of Grandmother Hoflund [Maria Larsdotter Spaak] I have no recollection. I think she passed away when about sixty years old. There were five children: three boys and two girls. Three of these children are buried in Henry County, Illinois.

My mother, [Anna Brita Carlsdotter] was born at Målen, Södra Vi Parish. Father and Mother went there on a visit when I was a little tot so young that they thought it impossible for me to have any remembrance of it. But when I told them, not long before Father died, that we went there on a sleigh; how the place looked; how the room where Grandpa was looked; that he was blind and was sitting on the side of the bed; they had to admit that I had some recollection of it. That was the only time I saw Mother's father, as he was quite old and died shortly after this visit. But of Grandma (on Mother's side) [Carolina Andersdotter] I have a more clear remembrance. She visited us while we lived in a place called Orremåla, and stayed quite a long time. From what I remember of her, she was not very amiable in her way, but rather self-willed and domineering. She looked strong and healthy, and lived to be quite old, although I have forgotten her exact age.

I think there were five children in the family, of which Mother was the youngest. I saw one of Mother's brothers a few times when I was very small, and I used to visit quite frequently at the home of one of her sisters. They lived not far from us when we lived in Djursdala, and every time I went there I would get a big slice of bread and butter. There were five children in this family—four boys and one girl. They did everything they could to entertain me, so it was a pleasure to go there on errands for mother, as I often did. All of that family came to this country at different times, except Uncle, who died in Sweden. They are now all dead except Erickson in

Moline, Illinois, and his elder brother Charles, who lives near Osceola, Nebraska.

I will now relate an experience I had in connection with these cousins. Uncle and Aunt were reputed to be very religious, more especially Uncle, and so he wanted the children to hear a certain wonderful minister who was to speak in a distant parish. They decided to go, and sent word for me to come and go along with them. After getting my parents' permission, I started for their home, Hillebo, on a Saturday afternoon in midwinter. In order to reach our destination in time for the services, we had to start from Hillebo at midnight. We did not dare go to bed, but sat up around the fireplace until it was time to start. When we went outdoors it was snowing, and as there was already considerable snow on the ground, it made the walking hard for the little tots. We were four in all; three boys and one girl, all about the same age.

Not far from home we had to cross Lake Krön, which was covered with ice and a deep layer of snow. It was not an easy matter for us to keep the track in the night, and the newly fallen snow had almost obliterated any trace of a path, so we were glad when we had crossed safely and came into the woods again, for there we had no difficulty in keeping the road, and then too, the wind was not so biting cold. Every moment we were getting more tired and wished more fervently that we had stayed at home. It must be remembered that in those days there were no such things as rubber overshoes or anything of that sort. All we had were little low shoes not much better than wooden ones, and every so often we would take them off and knock out the snow that had crowded in on the sides. I had no soft woolen underwear; nothing but a course, homespun linen shirt. In fact, all of my clothing was homespun and was very stiff and would sometimes chafe until the blood trickled down.

At daylight we came to a little hut in the pine woods near the road. We noticed that the people living there were up, as smoke was coming out of the chimney, so we concluded to go in and thaw out our lunch, rest a bit and have breakfast, which consisted of some black bread, cheese, and pork. These cottagers were very friendly and willing to let us share with them the comforts of their little fire in their rude, old-fashioned fireplace. This hospitality was a characteristic trait of these people all over Sweden.

After we had eaten and warmed ourselves we started on our journey for the final destination, Pelarne Church, which we reached soon after service had commenced.[3] Now we, of course, expected to have a great feast for our sin-sick little spirits, as well as rest for our sorely tired bodies. But in all this we were sorely disappointed, for we found the church packed with people to its utmost limits, and the temperature but little different from the outside, since the churches were not heated at that time (1848). There was no chance for a seat so we posted ourselves in the doorway, where we stood during the whole service, packed in like sardines, and had it not been that the pulpit was built out from the wall on the side of the church, we would not have had even a glimpse of the greatly renowned Pastor Ahlberg.[4] As near as I can figure it out (December 3, 1908), if I had never seen or heard him it would have been just as well for me, for I was not in a very receptive mood, and I don't think my young grandson, Stanley, under the same circumstances, would have been either. But I hope he will never have to put forth such strenuous efforts for such small results.

I don't remember a thing the good man said, but I am quite certain that the last word, "Amen," was the most satisfactory to me, especially as we had need of all the time that remained of that cold wintry Sunday to retrace that seemingly endless journey. It was certainly a test of endurance, and I think the last card was played when we arrived at Hillebo that Sunday night about twelve o'clock. Of course, the return trip was made toward home, and that word *home* is a wonderful stimulus for all people, though it be ever so humble.

Now the meditations that I have had on this episode have led me to the following conclusions: Would it not have been better for all concerned to have used a little common sense and given us, say five minutes, of good advice and ten minutes of kindly admonition. I know it would have been better for me, and I have reason to believe that my parents felt much the same way about it afterwards.

At this time we lived at Djursdala where we had moved after an absence of five years, during which time we had lived at a place called Orremåla, a few miles from Djursdala, but in the same parish. From Orremåla we moved to Frödinge and there we lived one year, which was one year too many for me, as I didn't like the place. From there we moved back to Djursdala about ten miles distant.[5] How glad I was when that 14th day of March came and I could start on that, to me, very important journey to Djursdala. The above date was the legal date for renters of farms to move, and Father was a renter.[6] I think Father had started the day before with the most of our possessions, and Mother and I were left alone to bring the balance the next day. We had a horse and a sleigh loaded with household goods, and an old black cow, who was so poor that for some time she had not been able to get up without help. We had but faint hopes of ever getting her to our destination that day, but expected to take her part of the distance at a time.

Mother was in the lead of the procession with some sliced raw potatoes, and a little meal in a pail, the cow followed, and the horse and myself brought up the rear. I was not the most experienced coachman at the age of seven and one-half years, but I managed to keep the road with no mishap. My greatest concern was to how long the cow would be able to keep on her legs. I imagine Mother had more or less concern for the whole caravan. When we had stretched the first mile behind us and the cow still on her pegs, how glad and thankful we were. As we proceeded farther and farther on our journey these feelings increased till at last we could hardly contain ourselves, for not only did the cow keep jogging along, but she actually seemed to be gaining in strength. It was to us a miracle for which we could not account. We did think, however, that the cow had been imbued with the same longing and desire to reach Djursdala that possessed us.

There is one incident which I was to relate before we leave Frödinge for good. In October of the fall we were there I was seven years old. Just about one week before Christmas, Father and Mother sent me and the hired girl to carry a grist of rye and wheat to the mill at Toverum, a nearby village. We started in the morning and got there about noon, but to our great disappointment when we arrived we found that the miller had just taken up the millstone and was dressing it, and he said that it would take him all afternoon. He told us we would have to go to another place farther on, and so we started again, and reached the mill in the afternoon. There were quite a number ahead of us. We were told that we would have to wait our turn, and that it would be quite late before they could get around to us.

Well, there was nothing else to do, so we waited till dark, although we were allowed to go into the miller's house for supper. It took us a good part of the night to get home, as the road led through the gloomy woods, and it was dark. About midnight I was so completely fagged out that I lagged behind, the hired girl continually urging me on. At last I could only make headway of a few rods at a time without a rest. Oh! but that little bag of flour was heavy. If I live to be a hundred years old I shall never forget the torment of that burden.

But I had some compensation when Yuletide came, and Mother presented me with a few little cakes out of that wheat flour. That was the only thing in the way of presents that I got any Christmas during the fifteen and one-half years I lived in Sweden. But I don't wish to convey the impression that I didn't have anything but hardships and gloom at Christmastime. On the contrary, we had the most enjoyable and happy time imaginable. Everybody was jubilant and glad, and tried to spread this happiness to everybody else even to the dumb brutes. Everyone was remembered in tokens of gratitude to Him who sent the world a Savior.

I don't feel competent to describe in detail the work of preparing for these festivities. For weeks everyone was busy. After the flax was prepared, spinning and weaving and knitting over, came the shoemakers and tailors, and then the brewing and distilling of the whiskey [*brännvin*], butchering and the making of sausages, and baking different kinds of bread, such as unbolted rye, which was the common everyday kind, "fine" bread, which was from bolted rye flour, and *limpa*, which was the same as the last mentioned, only made a little differently, and as a climax a few loaves of wheat bread. This baking was all done in a brick oven, and in quantity large enough to last for several months, and it wasn't hardtack [*spisbröd* or *knäckebröd*] either, for that wasn't used in our part of Sweden. Last but not least of these preparations comes the woodpile, which had to be of good size, the larger the better, and then too it had to be in good form. This part of the work fell to my lot the last two years we were there, and I entered into it with not a little enthusiasm.

It was quite a task, though, for a tot of my age to yoke up the oxen to a pair of bobs and go some distance to the place where the wood had been piled ready for winter use. As it was sometimes covered with snow two or three feet deep, it was difficult to find the wood and drive the oxen through the deep snow. It was not piled as cordwood is here, but cut off in lengths of about ten feet. Some of these logs were charred, and some were quite large, especially the hemlock, but as they were much lighter than pine or birch I selected them as much as possible, for they would elicit praise and wonder from all those who saw them, especially Mother, who would say, "But how in the world, child, could you load up such big logs and then raise them up on end in the woodpile?" The woodpile was in the shape of a pyramid, and I was not a little proud when I received this praise, for that was all the compensation I could ask.

It was customary to get up long before daylight on Christmas Eve morning, take a lantern or a torch and chop wood for the fireplace until time for breakfast. We were very careful to see that we had a good supply of hemlock for the evening, which would enliven the scene by its crackle like a lot of fire crackers.[7]

And now when the long and earnestly looked-for Christmas Eve had come, and the chores had been thoroughly attended to, which was not a small item, as the cow barn, horse barn, sheephouse, and even the hog house had to be cleaned, and the animals all given a double portion of the very best feed, we carried in the wood and got ready for the evening's pleasure.[8] Mother had different kinds of meat on the stone hearth (spishälla) before a roaring fire; not only did we have pork, beef, and mutton, but many different kinds of sausages and potatoes were placed there to roast. The whole hearth was full, and it was quite large, since it came out some distance from the wall in circular form and was about six inches higher than the floor.

Well, it was a scene, the impressions of which it is impossible for me to convey to an American-born, for it was a scene never witnessed in a common peasant's family but once a year. Generally in everyday life these things (meat, butter, cheese, and so forth) were meted out according to age. I was the oldest of the children and, for instance, when pork was served I generally got the largest piece of any of the children, and after that one piece it was useless to ask for more at that meal. But how gloriously everything had changed at Christmastime, for then and for sometime after we could have all we wanted of everything and anything there was. And then to sit down by a regular table, spread with a white linen cloth and lighted with candles, not a few, and the floor spread with pine and hemlock branches contributed not a little to the festivities.

Before we sat down to the table, Father would read out of a book of sermons, a part appropriate for the occasion, and then Mother and Father would sing some of those beautiful old Christmas hymns to be found in the Swedish Lutheran Hymn-book, which a Swede never tires of hearing. Both were good singers, and loved to sing, especially Mother who sang a great deal until she was ninety-one years old. She knew most of the Lutheran and Methodist hymnals by heart, and she would often sing while in bed at night, it was such a pleasure to her.[9]

All in all this Yuletide must have had a wonderful effect on us children, for I remember the last Christmas Eve we were in Djursdala going into the yard, and as I looked up into the sky on this clear starlit night, it seemed to me as though the whole heavens were full of music, and had come down so near to earth that the angels could be heard.

I have now tried to describe a Christmas in our part of the country among the farmer folk in 1848, and have gotten as far as about ten o'clock Christmas Eve. It was not thought best to stay up any longer, as we had to get up very early in order to go to *Julotta* [the Christmas morning service,] for up to this time it has been our physical being which has been cared for, and now comes the more important provision, that of our spiritual being. Of course, no one could rightly do that but our ordained rector, and in no other place could these needs be as effectively supplied as in the parish church. This was a rural district and some of the parishioners had to go five or six miles and even more on foot through the deep snow and bitter cold.

But regardless of all these difficulties everyone who was able to be up was sure to go to *Julotta*. They would have felt dissatisfied all the rest of the year if they had not gone. And think what a sight they would have missed. Every nook and corner of the old church was lighted with candles, the best lights of those days when there were no oil or kerosene lamps, and a church lighted by anything else than sunlight during the whole year with the exception of Christmas morning would have been out of all reason.

But I must not neglect to say something about our good rector, for he certainly was a picture worthy of the time and place. How we would stare at him in his brilliant vestments and a great glittering cross that covered his back. It was certainly something that would stir the dormant spirits that dwell inside those stiff, gray homespuns as nothing else could do.

A good part of the time was spent by us children in looking at the weird old fresco painting on the ceiling, which represented scenes of both Old and New Testaments, the prophets, evangelists, apostles, and a good sprinkling of angels good and bad. The pulpit was built out from the wall like a huge basket, so high that the head of an ordinary man was just visible. On top of this was placed a small, angelic figure, so it was not to be wondered at that in our estimation the man who occupied this important place was not an ordinary person, and for that reason, it was very natural that we should humble ourselves whenever he was met by taking off our caps and bowing very reverently.

Djursdala Church was, and is yet, a wooden structure, how old I never knew, and I believe, very few did know. Every seat [pew] had a door from the center aisle so that no one could get the seat they were not intended for. I think our seat was the third or fourth from the front, and I can remember that I had quite a little pride for being permitted to sit so near the altar, which was nicely decorated with a scene of the crucifixion.

Before I leave this subject I must say a few words about the old belfry, for it was always an object of interest to me. It was not connected with the church, but stood a little way off and was built a good deal on the plan of a windmill tower only very much higher and stronger. I think it had three bells. The largest one was larger than any I have ever seen since, and I remember it was said that it took a man with strong nerve to go up there in that rickety tower and ring the big bell. I was up in the belfry one time when this bell was rung, and have a very vivid recollection of how frightened I was when the man began to tread the big bell. The whole structure would sway, for the weight of the bells was below the beam or axle they were fastened to. I have learned recently that this tower and these bells were still standing at the present time, and they were doing service, which was a surprise to me, and I could hardly believe it.[10]

But I see I have digressed from my subject of Yuletide, so now a few words more about *Julotta*. Of course, everyone was anxious for the minister to come to the last words of his sermon as quickly as possible, and especially was this true of the younger generation. About the time the candles burnt down it began to get daylight, and then we could display our new clothes to good advantage. My, how anxious we children were that people would take notice of us and make some complimentary remarks.

As soon as services were over the young folks would break out for home to see who could get there first. Nearly everyone had to travel on foot, and when the snow was deep this task was quite a difficult one. The first thing we received on arriving home was a small glass of punch, which consisted of homemade whiskey [*brännvin*] diluted with water and sweetened to taste, some bread and butter, or a little cheese. Then we did the chores and had breakfast, after which the children would strike out for sport of some kind.

If the skating was good most all would steer for the mill pond or the low marshy ground along the river, as sometimes that would overflow and freeze and make the finest kind of a skating pond. When the weather was nice and the ice clear and smooth, we would keep it up all day and sometimes until late at night. I remember one time I was so tired and sore that I could hardly make my way home.

But if, as sometimes was the case, the snow had spoiled the skating, then we would have to resort to the toboggans or sleds, for there was always good sleighing during the winter. The road or street that ran through the hamlet [Djursdala village] was on quite a steep hill, and at the upper end, a little outside of the limits, was a still steeper hill. This was called *stentrappan*, which means stone stairs. Every hill, hillock, and mountain had its special name. At evening the young people would gather on top of this hill with sleds of all manner and fashion. The young men would press into service even bobsleds upon which all who had a chance would pile like a swarm of bees. Quite often someone would get hurt for the sled was sometimes so heavily loaded that it was hard to steer, and consequently they would run into a tree or a pile of boulders along the side of the road.

During this Christmastime there was a great deal of visiting, especially among relatives, and the visit would be not only for a single meal, but often for several days. So we certainly had a hilarious Christmastime in Sweden, and besides this there was a great number of festive days all of which contributed not a little to make the social conditions there very pleasant.

I will now try and describe, as well as I can, the little hamlet of Djursdala, where I spent the most, as well as the happiest, time of my life in Sweden. The place and its surroundings consisted of four *hemman*, which means homestead, and these homesteads were divided up between thirty or thirty-two farmers. Father rented one-quarter homestead, but a far greater number had much less. The land was not divided up into quarter sections as it is in the United States, so a homestead did not signify a certain number of acres, for it would contain more or less area, depending largely on the quality of the soil and so forth.[11]

Through the center of the village ran the main road, and instead of the living [dwelling] houses being built so as to face the road they were placed quite a way back and all of the outbuildings were built on a line with a driveway from the street into an open court or barnyard. Around this court was built the cow barn (*kohuset*), horse barn (*stallet*), sheephouse (*fårahuset*), hay barn (*lada*), and a barn where all the grain was housed and threshed. This was the largest building, and here we had a threshing floor on which the threshing was done with flails.

We would get up at one or two o'clock in the morning and thresh until daybreak, when we would have something to eat, do the chores, and the men would hitch up the oxen and start to the timber for the day's work. For two or three years I had to be along more or less all of the time and do what I could, and it was by no means a pleasant task to get up at that time in the morning in the middle of winter. But such was the custom, if not the necessity, that inflicted such unseemly hardships.

Besides the above-enumerated buildings, there was the wagon and tool house, which was built in a quadrangle around the barnyard. All of the places were built much on the same plan, with two or three other buildings nearer the living house, such as the granary, where was kept not only the grain that was raised on the farm, but many things in the culinary line, [such] as flour, meat, and all things not easily damaged by frost.

Then there was the brewhouse, where we brewed the beer as well as our homemade whiskey [*brännvin*], for nearly every farmer of those days had a small still and made his own whiskey, and though young, I had to sit up many a night and watch the still.[12] This task I did not much enjoy, since one could not help meditating on those terrible stories of ghosts and goblins that were so persistently told and believed by nearly everybody. Then too, there was no light save a dull flicker from the fire under the still. It was certainly a dark, weird, and gloomy place, and the least bit of noise sent a cold shiver through me, and every nook and corner seemed to be possessed by some unearthly being.

There was one other building in the belongings of a well-ordered farm, which was placed quite a distance from the other buildings on account of danger from fire, and was used principally for drying flax. The one we had was a low, square building built of round logs, the seams caulked up with moss or clay. In the center an oven was built of wood or stone in which we kept a fire, and as there was no chimney, we could not go in until the wood was charred because of the smoke. All around the sides were bunks and here the flax was stored to dry. There was not a little work connected with this preparation of flax before it was transformed into different kinds of fabric for wearing apparel.

Now a few words about fruit. Nearly every farm had more or less fruit, such as apples, pears, cherries, of which of the latter there were many varieties and of the best quality — equal to, if not better than, the California cherries. They had no use for the more tarty kinds of cherries, for sugar was a luxury which but comparatively few could afford. When we moved to Djursdala, I planted some cherry seeds, and one of the trees from those seeds had cherries on before we moved away (seven years). We had one apple tree in our yard, and we called it [in local dialect] *kreskapla* (tart apple). This tree was loaded with fruit, but would bear only every other year.

We also had currants, gooseberries, strawberries, blueberries, and red whortleberries. There were several kinds of plums on our farm, but no peaches or wild fruits of any kind. The whortleberries [*lingon*] were much like cranberries, and grew in one compact bunch. They would keep all winter the same as cranberries, and as they were very plentiful, we always laid in a good supply. Next in abundance to whortleberries were the blueberries. I have a very vivid recollection, in connection with this, of an incident that caused me much sorrow at the time, and of which I have never been fully relieved even in after years.

While we were living in Djursdala some of my sisters and I went out to pick blueberries on what was to me one of the most gloomy days of which I have any recollection. We went to a place called *Halshagen* (Horse Pasture), and from there to *Djupadaln* (Deep Valley). This was a very dreary spot, lying in between two rugged mountains. A part of it was marshy, and to heighten the extreme dreariness of the place, if that were possible, the stories we had heard of goblins, elfs, and spirits kept continually arising before us, for these evil beings were supposed to infest this region. They lived in the mountains, according to popular traditions, and would manifest themselves to people who happened to pass through late in the evening or at night. All of these things, and more, we children had heard and, of course, believed, for we could not disprove them. On this particular day we thought we heard all kinds of noises and rustlings, saw any number of snakes, and heard low, distant thunder in the mountains. In aftertime I have been inclined to believe that it was a kind of foreboding of what was to happen at the close of day.

We arrived home about dusk, and as our parents were some distance away at work (they were binding birch twigs to be fed to the sheep in the winter), I started to chop kindling in the vestibule of the house in order to make a fire in the fireplace. I used for this a kind of light, broad ax and a chopping block. It was quite dark and I did not see my youngest sister (she was not quite four years old) crawl round and reach for a chip. But as the ax fell it struck her left hand and nearly chopped it off. It cut clear through the palm, leaving her only the use of the forefinger. When I heard her scream and caught a glimpse of her hand dangling by the skin, I was nearly frightened to death. I first ran to a neighbor woman, and then to where I thought the folks were working, but I met them as they were coming home. I was so excited I could not stay with them, but bolted right back, went upstairs, and crawled under the bed and stayed there until Mother was through with her work and came up and consoled me. But this unfortunate accident cast a gloom over me, which, for a long time, weighed very heavily. Since then, whenever I have thought of my sister Charlotte it has been with a pang of sorrow. She died in 1899 and was laid to rest in the Swedish Methodist Episcopal cemetery at Andover, Henry County, Illinois.

I will now relate a little incident that will in a measure

show to what extent the people were affected by these stories of goblins and elfs. I think it was the last summer we were in Djursdala, during haying time, we went one morning to this same place, *Djupadaln*, of which I gave a short description. As it was quite a distance from home, something was taken along for dinner so that we could stay all day, and cut and gather up what little hay there was in among the rocks. There was also some grass on the wet, marshy places that had to be brought onto the dry land. When noon came we had our nap, which was customary, since the days were long and the nights short in that latitude at that time of year. Well, Mother lay down on a flat stone which was a little above the ground on a small pile of rocks. When she got up she said she felt rather peculiar, but we worked the rest of the day, went home, and thought no more about it. She, however, began to grow worse, and after a week or two we became very uneasy about her condition.

Of course, we did not think of going for a doctor, for that was not the custom (I don't believe I ever saw a doctor on a professional call while in Sweden), but it was evident something must be done. The most peculiar thing about it was her hair was so tangled and knotty that she could hardly comb or do anything with it. Mother finally came to the conclusion that she had, in some way, offended these elfs, who were believed to live in the valley, and we decided to visit the very spot where Mother had taken her nap that day when out haying.

She told Father of her plan and asked him to go along; but as he had very little faith in these stories of ghosts and goblins and their wonderful powers, he would put her off from time to time. But her condition at last became so serious that he consented to accompany her, and one Sunday morning quite early, fortified with a hymnbook, they started on their mission of conciliation. Sure enough, incredible as it may seem, from that time she began to get better in the ratio that she had been getting worse, and in about three weeks she had regained her usual good health.

A great many of the poorer class had to send their children out begging, and Mother would always give them something, even if it was only a few potatoes. Quite often a journeyman of some kind of trade would come and ask for something to eat. These men were of a privileged class, for when they had served their apprenticeship they were given a license to travel, and I believe it was mandatory that they should travel before they were authorized to settle down and do business on their own account.[13]

One of them came to our house one afternoon and asked to stay overnight and Father consented. Well, in the evening a couple of neighbors came in. One of them was a vicious character, a leader of the bad element in the place, overbearing and abusive. We were all sitting around the fireplace, the journeyman at one side. After a while this rowdy began to pick a quarrel with the stranger, calling him abusive names, but through it all the man kept quiet. Finally he got so abusive that Father told him to stop, but he paid no attention, and then Father told him he would have to quit his abuse of a man who was under our roof and entitled to our protection.

Then the ruffian jumped up and into the middle of the room and blurted out: "*Vad säger du, bonddjavul?*" ("What have you got to say, farmer devil?"). At that Father grabbed him by the coat collar and there they stood for a few seconds, Mother and the children scared to death and screaming. But all of a sudden there was a great commotion and a crash at the door of the vestibule, where our unruly visitor picked himself up and hurled vile epithets at Father as he disappeared in the dark. He did not even come back for his watch, which he lost in the struggle, and so the journeyman was left in peace.

We were very much afraid for some time after that the rowdy would do some mischief to Father, for he was the leader of a tough crowd and had many chums, one of whom was very much infatuated with a cousin of mine. My uncle and aunt were very much opposed to this match. They could not get rid of the young fellow, for the girl thought much of him. This was a wonder to the neighbors for she was much superior to him, both in station and person.

One day Uncle Nils came to have a talk with Father and solicit his aid in breaking up the match if possible, and, as Father had no particular liking for the man, he readily consented to do what he could. So one day when this young man came there, Father went in and after a while the fellow came out with Father after him. I remember how scared I was that there would be a fight. He kept away from Father, walking backwards all the way out to the barnyard, and after he had gone through the gate Father came back and that was the end of it. He never came back again, and my cousin finally married another man, David Peterson, and after a few years they came to this country and settled near Orion, Henry County, Illinois. They are both buried in the Lutheran cemetery at Orion, Illinois.

I will now relate an incident that happened while we were in Djursdala, which will throw some light on the morals of the place. At that time a new minister came to our parish from some distant neighborhood, and so of course he was a stranger to many things in our region. It was said that he was a very learned man and high toned. After a while he heard how the young folks carried on, especially on Sundays, and he resolved that he would put a stop to it. So he gave warnings from the pulpit that they quit gambling, dancing, and so forth on Sunday. However, this was without the desired effect, and he finally gave notice from the pulpit to the young men that they must appear before him at the parsonage on a certain day.

When the day came they were all ready. They went on horseback, dressed up like clowns with scarfs, belts, and their hats or caps turned inside out, and armed with all kinds of instruments, such as drums and horns. The leader had a jug full of whiskey and they seemed to glory in that, for it was very prominent in the display. It was said that when they arrived at the parsonage, they rode into the orchard and tied their horses to the fruit trees and then went in in a body. It is hardly to be expected that the minister was prepared for any such scene of wickedness, and it is very likely that when they came away they prided themselves on having gained a great victory over their pastor.

For a time there was nothing more heard of this but the good and learned man was not to be defeated with one encounter, so he gave them another call to come on a certain day, and when that day arrived they went much in the same way as before, only this time they went in wagons and had a keg of whiskey very prominently placed on a platform. Well, they came back and as far as I know this was the end of the incident for everything seemed to go on as before. It gave the place a harder name than it really deserved, for aside from this rowdy element of a comparative few, the people were peaceable and law abiding. Although they had many things in common, they got along very nicely and it was with reluctance that we left and went to Orremåla.

Orremåla was a small hamlet of five or six families, but a much nicer place than Djursdala. It was better built and the scenery was fine, the town [i.e., hamlet] being surrounded with meadows. We had a nice orchard and not far away was a lake that supplied us with fresh fish now and then. Orremåla was not a strange place to us, for we had lived there three years before, and the man who owned the place father rented was a distant relative of ours. The farm had good pasture- and hay-lands, but was not so good for grain as the land we left.

About this time quite a number of families had emigrated to America, and had written back from time to time. These letters would circulate and be read until they were so soiled and worn that it was difficult to read them. I was the only one who could read these letters, and they seemed to have a marked effect on those who heard them, for they were the cause of a great number leaving and going to America. About this time I came across a little book which contained something about Indians and Niagara Falls. It was wonderfully interesting reading for me, and part of it I remember to this day.[14]

Frugality entered into everything, but we could not get along without some money and it was customary to do some freighting. We hauled iron ore to the smelters, also glass bottles from a glass factory some distance from our home to a place called Westervik [now spelled Västervik], on the Baltic Sea about forty miles from Orremåla. One Tuesday in the winter of 1850 it was planned that I should go to the glass factory after a load of glass bottles, but for some reason it was put off and I did not go. This was very lucky for me, for about the middle of the day a blizzard came up, the worst any of the old timers had seen, and to this day this is known as the "Blizzardy Tuesday." Many people froze to death, as well as great numbers of horses and oxen that happened to be out teaming. They would get stuck in a drift and that was the end; so I always regarded it as providential that I was kept at home that day.

At this time we had two good horses and one good yoke of oxen. We did considerable freighting during the winter, but for all that I thought I could see it was nip-and-tuck for us to hold our own, and when I cast my thoughts into the future to try and see what there was in store for me, I did not find the prospects very bright. Instead my future would be full of hard and gloomy struggles. I pictured to myself a little cot on some out-of-the-way, lonely, gravel knoll, for which I would have to work a certain length of time before securing [it] for myself. These thoughts and pictures occupied my mind not a little and did not contribute to a happy and contented life.

In the fall I was sent to do some plowing in a stubble field with a yoke of oxen, which was not an easy task for a lad of my age (I was fifteen that fall), as the ground was very stony. Large boulders on the surface and underneath would cause the plow handle to land in the stomach, which would get mighty sore after a few hard thumps. But I was getting along quite well for it was work that I liked, but all of a sudden I had an experience which is hard for me to describe, though I remember it as well as if it had happened yesterday. While I was working along, it seemed to me as though I was enveloped in a dark cloud and such gloomy feelings that came over me have never been experienced before or since. It seemed to me it was a power from some source compelling me to quit my work. Resolving with all my might to take whatever consequences, but never to plow another furrow, I unhitched the oxen from the plow, went home, put the oxen in the barn, and then went into the house where Mother was sitting at the loom weaving. I told her of my resolve never to go back to that field, even if Father whipped me blue.

"I will never go back, never, never, never."

Well, she commenced to cry and said, "Dear, child, what is the matter with you?"

"Nothing, only I will never go back there to work as long as I live," and I never did and was never asked to do so. That was the last plowing for me in Sweden. My next was in Clover Township, Henry County, Illinois.

Sometime after this Father and Mother began talking America. Father said he had had a similar experience to mine. He was in the timber chopping down a hemlock and he had it about half down when he quit and went home. From this time on our thoughts were more earnestly turned towards America, but it was not a thing easily decided, for all that was known by the common people was what we had learned from the letters of those who had gone, and they contained much that was hard to believe. At this time just a few had gone from our neighborhood, I believe one or two families, and they located near Andover, Henry County, Illinois.[15] I remember reading the letters they sent their relatives, in which they made a statement of how many pounds of pork a man was offered for a day's work, and it was nearly unbelievable to us peasants in Sweden that so much could be paid for one day's labor.[16]

Finally, however, we decided once and for all to go to America. There were six children in the family, all rugged and healthy, but it required not a little resolution to overcome the difficulties, real and imaginary. Even if we succeeded in getting across, what would we find or what new troubles would be awaiting us? We had means enough to take us there, but very little more and this also worried us not a little. As soon as it was known that Father had decided to go to America there was an onslaught from relatives and friends, begging and protesting with tears not to go, and picturing all manner of calamities to which we might be exposed. So it required a great deal of courage to give up what was considered a good thing for an uncertainty, to leave a place that had supported us and our forebears for generations, and not a kith or kin had ever left it for unknown and strange pastures.

But from this time America was uppermost in our thoughts and conversation, and before winter was over two other families in our parish had decided to go along. Also father's sister and brother-in-law with their two children reached the same conclusion, and so it was quite a little company when we got together. The last work I did in Sweden with the oxen was to haul a load of wood to a couple of poor woman cottagers [*torpare*], who were sisters and also invalids. I remember how sorry they were to have us leave, for father and mother had always been so good to them.

There is one incident which befell shortly before we left Sweden and I will tell it here. My Uncle L. M. Hoflund had many children with whom I played a great deal. Their youngest son was a year older than I, and, naturally, we became great friends. At the time this accident took place he was fifteen years old, and was able to do almost anything a man could. His father was burning two charcoal pits quite a distance apart, and he would leave his son, Nils Johan, at one while he would go back and forth. I can't say how long it took him to burn a *kolmila* [charcoal kiln], but it must have been a week or more. One night while the boy was alone he went out on the pit to see if it was all right, and as he went he fell into an opening the full length of the pit. I don't remember how his father found out about it, but he must have made some noise or cried for help. This cast a gloom over the whole community, and the boy's father did not live but a short time, for this tragedy grieved him to death. These two funerals were the saddest I ever attended. I have an infant brother buried near this uncle and cousin.

# 2

# The Journey to America,

# 1850

Ajourney from Sweden in those days was somewhat different than it is today, so it was no wonder that our minds were occupied with all kinds of forebodings. The last work that I remember of doing in Sweden was to help an old cottager peel off some hemlock bark for tanning.

I can't remember the date we left Sweden but it was in the spring of 1850. Nor can I remember any incident upon leaving Orremåla, but when we came to Djursdala [village] the whole place turned out to bid us good-bye, and a goodly number followed us for some distance. Many of Father's friends pleaded with him to promise to come back. When they turned to go, Father called out to them that in ten years they could look for him, and that was our parting word to the old home in Sweden. We had now cut loose from our old familiar surroundings and were on our way to the great unknown.

At noon, on the first day, we met my uncle and aunt and their two children, and were very glad to meet them. At Berg we were to part with the last of our friends and old neighbors, Uncle Johannes Hoflund and an old friend whose name I have forgotten. I have a very vivid recollection of that parting, for it was about the saddest I ever experienced. For this was the last cord that held me to old and dear memories, and from here we must set forth alone.[1] Oh! but I felt sad, for I thought so much of Uncle Johannes. He was Father's youngest brother, and I used to spend much of my time at their home while we lived in Djursdala.

Up to Motala there are fifteen locks in the [Göta] canal, so we had time to see the factory, and among other things to be seen there, a trip hammer, the largest in Europe. It was called *Wrede*.[2] Between Motala and Lake Venern [now spelled Vänern] there are many pretty scenes. It was now late in the day, and when we got to the lake it had clouded up and started to rain. It was quite chilly for that time of year and we had no cover over us. The only covered place, as I recollect, was a passageway between the boiler and the railing, the fore and aft being open. Of course this was on the deck. They had cabins below, but that was not for us. As we got out onto the lake, the wind arose to quite a height and it wasn't long before we began to feel pretty sick, all of us, I believe, with the exception of my brother Alexander. Mother was terribly sick, and she called me to her and said she would die.

"Oh! that I had stayed at home. I would have worked my fingernails off to earn a living. Dear child, if you can, but I'm afraid you can't, hunt up the lunch box for me."

It was now quite dark and I didn't know exactly where it was, but between my own sick spells I went to work and finally found the box and a bottle of brandy. That seemed to strengthen her some, but she said, years afterward, she really believed she would have died if she hadn't received that stimulant. Everything was gloomy enough as it was, but to make it still worse Father was forced to stay behind and care for Uncle Lawerence [Lars], who was quite sick and prevented from going with the rest. There were eight children, Mother and Aunt sick, and no place for which to aim with any satisfaction of bettering our conditions.

Well, after crossing Lake Venern, we finally came to Trollhättan. There were many locks, I think seventeen, and we had plenty of time to view the grand scenery. We went up to *Toppö* (Top Island), from which the view was beautiful. I have no recollection of any scenery between Motala and Gothenburg.[3] This trip was probably made at night.

Now the question was what were we to do and where were we to go when we got to Gothenburg.[4] Everything was strange, we knew no one, we had no experience to help, Father left behind, Mother still sick, and consequently it was a gloomy outlook confronting us. But by the help of someone, we were conducted to the harbor and found the sailing vessel *Virginia* (Captain E. A. Jansson), and were put aboard. We were allowed to stay there while they were putting on the cargo of bar iron.[5]

I don't remember how long it was before Father came, but it must have been several weeks, and during all that time Mother was very depressed, crying continually. Finally, however, one day Father came, and with him Uncle Lawerence, who was still sick. He had to be taken to a hospital and there he stayed until he died. I don't remember how long we stayed in Gothenburg. I never heard Mother say and she was the one who kept the records in her mind, for she had a remarkable memory.

There were six of us children. I was the oldest, in my fifteenth year. The sister next to me was Caroline, then Mary, then Johanna and Lottie and my brother, Alexander. My aunt had two children; the oldest was Josephine and then Albert Håkan.[6] Everything we saw in Gothenburg was very interesting to us children as we had never been away from home and had not seen any large place. We would stroll out as far as we dared and sometimes would even make up a party and cross the river to the island of Hisingen, which was rocky and barren. Here and there a little fisherman's cottage could be seen with a scrawny garden around it, but on the whole there was not much of beauty in the surroundings.

I can't remember how long we stayed in Gothenburg, but we left on the twenty-first day of June, 1850. This is a copy of the receipt we received from the ship company:

Passage fare to New York by the ship, *Virginia*, Captain E. A. Jansson. I have this day received from landholder G. P. Hoflund, wife and six children, a sum amounting to 275 ricksdaler banco, which is hereby receipted.
Gothenburg, the 21st of June, 1850.
Olaf Wyke,[7]
H. P. Matern.

On leaving we entered the ocean through Gothenburg harbor. We now depended upon the winds for our motive power to push us ahead. Everything went all right, although more or less fear possessed us. It had been rumored that the ship *Virginia* was condemned by the authorities as unseaworthy. It had plied between Gothenburg and New York for many years, but the captain they said was safe as he was a good and careful man.[8] As we passed on into the ocean, while I was standing on deck I looked back and what a wonderful feeling arose with the thought that it was the last sight I would have of my native land. The horizon presented a blue line of rocks, with no trees to break the jagged outline.

That was the last sight of land until we reached the harbor of New York, after one day less than two months of voyage and sky and water. It got to be pretty monotonous, and some of us were sick all of the time. The only ones who were not sick were Father and my youngest brother. For some time nothing unusual happened, but after sailing some days we were overtaken by a calm, and for three days we lay becalmed and did not move in any direction. The surface of the water was as smooth as glass, and every here and there would be great schools of fishes, and in the distance we would often see huge whales spouting water in the air thirty or forty feet.

I was sick more or less all of the time for the two months, and what I lived on I can't imagine, for we had nothing much to eat. Father bought a lot of hardtack, I don't know what it was made of, but we didn't relish it, to say the least. We had to get our own meals, but did not have a place to cook coffee or anything else. I remember a firkin of anchovies, and the sight of it would make me sick for the balance of my days, and to this day if I see a firkin in a store I have to turn away from it. We had no coffee, not a pound of butter, nor any canned goods of any kind. I believe one good meal would have cured me of all my sickness. One cup of coffee would have fixed me all right, but as far as I remember I only had two cups of coffee all of the time I was in Sweden. The sailors, of course, had a cook and a small stove, but no one was allowed to use it, and even if [we] had been we didn't have anything to cook.

For a time we made no headway and it seemed as though we would never get through with the voyage, but towards the last we had a heavy wind which developed into a regular gale. Then we thought we were gone for sure. The waves rolled mountain high, and it seemed almost impossible that the ship could ride them. The ship was loaded with iron clear up to the deck and the sailors crawled in between the deck and the iron. They were scarcely able to get through with the lanterns in order to see if the props were in place. They said if the props gave way the iron would begin to slide and our fate would be sealed.

I don't remember how long this wind kept up, but it was favorable and sent us hurrying along towards our destination. So a short time after this storm we had the glad tidings that we were nearing land and this to us was wonderful news. It is impossible to describe the feelings which were aroused. We could hardly bring ourselves to believe that it was true. Some of the passengers had been in bed nearly all of the time, for we had some families along who were quite old and in bad shape.

Everything seemed to come true with me as I had expected. We left barren rocks and here we found tree-covered shores, and to me it looked pretty and inviting. We got a pilot aboard, but we did not have to stop in quarantine. I don't remember the exact number of passengers but it was not very many, as there was room for a very few.[9]

When we came into port we began to realize that we were in a country where our language was no good to us. At that time there were very few Swedes in America.[10] Father went ashore to see if he could find someone who could give us the information we needed. He was referred to Captain Erickson, who, I think, was the same man who invented the famous little *Monitor* that cut such a prominent figure in the Civil War.[11] What little money we had, had to be changed, and we took a steamboat on the Hudson for Albany.

I don't remember how long we stayed in New York City, but it could not have been more than a day or two. When our things finally were carted over to the steamer and we all got aboard, Father was missing and then we had some excitement. Mother and Aunt were nearly beside themselves, but just as the last bell was ringing he came poking along just in the nick of time.

While we were in New York I remember going with several others to what was called the Bethel Ship where Rev. Haedstrom was holding forth as a Methodist minister for the few Swedes in the city and for the seafaring people. He was the first Swedish minister in this country.[12] I saw him afterwards in Chicago, twenty-three or -four years later. From what I saw and heard of him in Chicago, I will always remember, for he was a grand old man. The last time I saw him was when I had gone to Chicago with our minister to represent our church in the Sunday School Convention. The Norwegians and Swedes were trying to start a school together and Haedstrom was elected chairman of the convention. He had many an anecdote of his experiences, which were always very interesting to me. I remember he told us that his health had been failing, but that he had a strong desire to go back to the Old Country once more. He said that he prayed to God to give him strength and health. He had a little altar in his backyard where he used to go a certain time each day and plead with God.

"And from that time forth, I have been as strong and healthy as you see me now," and he jumped up and down like a young colt.

Sometime in the evening we started for Albany, and we had to huddle together as best we could on the deck. I remember peeping into the cabin on this boat, and to me it seemed as though a heaven had been opened. Next morning we arrived at Albany, and there we were in for another change from the steamboat to a canal boat, which was pulled along by horses on the shore.[13]

I have no recollection of how long it took us to travel from Albany to Buffalo, but I remember some of the experiences we had. The country looked good to us, and we were glad we were not on the ocean, but there was a great deal of sickness that made it very unpleasant. Then we had no place to stay but down in the hull of the boat among the boxes and barrels, and hardly anything to live on. When we arrived at the locks some of the girls would leave the boat and go to a farmer's house, and come back ladened with good things, such as pie and cake and bread and everything you can imagine and we would live high for a time. A good many complained of the bread tasting salty, but to me it was manna from heaven, for my stomach had had a long rest and anything tasted fine.

From Buffalo we got a steamboat, which was to land us in Chicago. We were favored with good weather on the Lakes, and if a wind should have come up, I am sure we would have capsized, for the crew of the boat was kept busy a good deal of the time rolling scrap iron barrels from one side of the ship to the other in order to keep the proper balance. At times the boat would scuttle to one side and everyone was panic stricken.

When we arrived in Chicago, we hunted up a family who had emigrated one year before and had settled in Chicago. Their name was Speake. How we found them I am at a loss to know, but I remember going there one afternoon. We crossed the Chicago River on a raft, since there were no bridges then as there are now. These people were distant relatives of ours, and, like most of the emigrants, were very poor.[14] Nevertheless we were glad to be with someone who could talk with us, and who had picked up a little knowledge of this country.

We did not stay in Chicago but a short time, and as it appears to me now it was not a very inviting place. It was flat and low and the streets were planked. The houses were built upon isolated blocks separated by vacant lots, and all this tended to make the place look very peculiar. There were quite a number of inhabitants but they were scattered over a wide area.[15]

When we were ready to leave Chicago we took a canal boat to La Salle and stayed there one night. Cholera was raging and many fell victims to it, and, I believe, some of our number died at La Salle.[16]

Father hired a team here to take us over the country to Andover, Henry County, Illinois. One of the men of our party, Steinholm by name, had taken a wagon with him thinking that it would be an improvement upon what the people had here in the way of wagons.[17] When we got to La Salle he couldn't very well load it up with trunks, so he had to buy a horse for the wagon, and he finally bought a bobtailed outlaw that ran away every chance he got and lots of times when he didn't get a chance. We loaded the wagon with sacks, trunks, and bundles to its utmost capacity, and all who were able had to walk, especially uphill.

I think the first day's drive brought us to Princeton, Bureau County, Illinois, and here some of our party left us. We stayed overnight, but I have not a very clear remembrance of the place or its surroundings. After leaving Princeton, the next day we were driving through an open prairie and on a long downslope. I happened to look up and saw Tufting, who was driving the outlaw, coming a mile-a-minute, and the bobtail was putting in his very best licks and everything was sailing fine until they came bumping into our wagon. Our wagon was upset, and we went sprawling to the ground in a most undignified manner. Everything was pandemonium, and we were nearly frightened to death. It was a wonder that none of us were injured, for the horses and all took a header.

Although I have no distinct recollection, I believe we stopped on our last night somewhere near Kewanee. I remember very distinctly coming into Cambridge. Cambridge had been made the county seat of Henry County only a short time before this, and it contained only a few buildings. There was one store, kept by a Mr. Gaines, and the courthouse which was a two-story frame building, and had been moved from Morristown. That was the courthouse in which Eric Johnson had been murdered the summer before by a man named Root, whose wife was a member of the Bishop Hill Colony.[18] From Cambridge we had only a few miles to Andover, and we arrived there in the afternoon of the first day of October, 1850.

Andover was nothing but a name. Our freighter said,

"There is Andover." On the south was the white-oak grove, and in every direction was the vast extending prairie. Father had expected to find something of a place and he objected to being dumped off on the open prairie, but finally through a Swede, who happened to be working nearby, he learned that this spot was really Andover.[19] We unloaded and in the course of the afternoon we found a Swede widow-lady who lived nearby. This widow was the mother of Congressman Lobeck.[20] We were allowed to take our possessions into her yard, and there, under the trees of the locust grove, we stayed all night.

# 3

# Early Days on the Illinois Prairie,

## 1850–1851

There was a man named Lobeck, who was staying on this farm who afterwards married the widow. The next morning, which was the first for me in Andover, a man came in, who said he wanted a boy or young man to do some work for him on the farm. Someone pointed me out and the result was that I went with him. His name was Stoddard, and I worked with him about a year. I have reason to be thankful for this opportunity because I was in a good family and they treated me very fine.

I now had a chance to take a ride in an American farm wagon. In driving along the wind would blow the fly nets, which were made of muslin, up over the horses' backs. I didn't think that looked right, and so I climbed over the dashboard while the horses were going and straightened them out. Well, I could see the old gentleman smile, but he let me do it a few times and then motioned that I did not need to bother with them anymore. Mr. Stoddard lived about four miles south of Andover in Oxford township. We arrived home about noon, and after putting up the horses we went in to dinner. That was the first time I had sat down to a spread table since we left Sweden, and was the first square meal I had had since we left.

But now I was brought up against the fact that I couldn't

make myself understood. I realized now what it was to be in a foreign country and away from home. I had never been away from home before, and had scarcely even been away from my parents. I did not even know how to say yes or no in the language, and when the family tried to talk with me I was very much embarrassed. Finally, I made out that they wanted to know whether I had any brothers or sisters, and I held up my fingers as a sign that I had five.

After dinner Mr. Stoddard sent me with his two sons, both younger than I, to help herd some cattle that were feeding in a neighboring pasture. That was my first occupation in America. But I made good use of those two boys that afternoon in trying to pick up some words. My store, however, was just as meager at night as it had been at noon, and it made me feel discouraged. When I left my parents, I did not know where they were going or what they were going to do, so that was also a source of great discouragement to me.

I don't remember what kind of work I was engaged in that fall, but I remember one day I went with the family to pick crab apples near Bishop Hill, on the Edwards River Bottoms. I also remember having to do the chores and herd the sheep, of which Mr. Stoddard had quite a number. He did not have a large farm, only forty acres, and that was not all broken. Chopping firewood occupied a good deal of my time, which wasn't such unpleasant work.

Sometime during the year a party of movers came through and stopped at Stoddard's overnight. I sat and listened to their conversation and would sometimes make up my mind to catch even a single word, and though I sat for hours, I never could make out a single expression. Having made up my mind to master the language, I was sometimes able to associate some word with a particular thing and that way I acquired a little understanding of American expressions. The further I advanced in this the easier it was for me, and in a short time it seemed to me the language came quite fast, so that when I had been there a year I felt I could talk as plainly as a native-born.

Sometime during the fall a man drove up in front of our place with a horse and buggy. I was told that he was a Swede, and Mr. Stoddard went out and talked with him. The man's name was Jonas Haedstrom, a Methodist Episcopal minister and a brother to the Rev. Haedstrom we met in New York City.[1] After Mr. Stoddard left him, I had a talk with him and among other things, I asked him about the pay I would receive while working for him. No amount had been decided upon and I was worried about it considerably. He told me I didn't need to worry about the salary because I was working for an honest family.

I didn't let that matter worry me, and after I had gone to Minnesota Mr. Stoddard paid Father at the rate of four dollars a month for the winter and six dollars for the summer. I had a good home here and afterwards wished that I had stayed, for it would have saved me some of the hardest knocks of my life. I also would have had a chance for some schooling.

When harvesttime came Mr. Stoddard had his grain cut, and we bound it up afterwards whenever we had time. He hired his brother-in-law and another man to help in this work, and I was put to binding by myself. I wasn't accustomed to the way they bound and so progressed rather slowly. But Mr. Stoddard taught me how to make the band and tie the knot and then left me to work out my own salvation. This was in the afternoon, and I worked away until I could tie up the bundles pretty lively. A day or two later we went over to a neighbor's to bind oats and then I went in with the rest of them. We took a row apiece, went abreast, and when I found that I could keep up with the rest of them I felt pretty elated.

The next day I went to bind for a man by the name of

Jennings. He had a patch of forty acres of wheat cut, and he called in the young men of the neighborhood and held a "bee." I don't remember how many there were, but the intention was to bind that wheat field that day, so there must have been quite a number, and I bound abreast of the rest of them.

Sometime during that afternoon a man, James Kramer, about twenty years of age, began bantering me for a race, and he kept at it so persistently that I got a little nettled, and said, "All right, here goes," and we started in and kept it up for one round of forty acres. It was pretty hot work but I came out one or two bundles ahead. Well, that cooled him off a little, and made me feel pretty good, for I was only seventeen and had only bound for a few days. He wasn't satisfied and so challenged me again. He took the outside row this time, and we went another round and by the time we made the round we had caught up with the rest, or in other words, we made two rounds while they were making one, and I beat him several rows.

Then Daniel Kramer challenged me and we had only gone a few rods on this, my third race, when he said, "That's enough, this is too fast a pace for me," so I was the cock of the pit, and as I was also the youngest I am afraid that the young, green Swede swelled up a little more than he ought to have done. But at any rate it encouraged me quite a bit to see that I was as good as the rest of the men. I don't think I was ever beaten by anyone in a binding contest.

I remember working for a Mr. Smith, an uncle of C. O. Lobeck, the congressman from Omaha. He had a large harvest, and I worked there twenty days, and he had quite a large crew of men during that whole time. Sometimes some of the men would take a notion they would show us how to bind and whenever I saw one start I took after him and it wasn't but a short time until I had him in the rear. There was a Swedish woman, Mrs. Danielson, in the crew and she started out one day and I gave chase, and she finally gave in, although we were neck and neck nearly all of the way.

After I was through with Smith, Lobeck hired me and this same woman was in the crew. She still had the notion that she could beat me. We went in for it and she really gave me the worst race I ever had, and I won only by a short distance.

In harvesttime we were paid a dollar a day, which was considered big money then. I liked the work and felt I could keep at it all of the time, although it was very hard on some. A good many lost their lives during the hot weather at that kind of work. One night at Smith's we missed a man at the supper table, and when we went out with lanterns to hunt for him, we found him dead. He had been overcome with the heat.

When I left Stoddard's it was against his wishes, as he wanted me to stay with him until I was twenty-one. There was never a word said during all this time about wages, but afterwards it was settled satisfactorily with Father. I don't see how they could pay me even what they did, for I had such a raving appetite that I shouldn't have thought there would be anything coming to me. In the wintertime when there was not much work they had only two meals a day, but they told me that anytime I felt like it I could go to the cupboard and help myself, but I never took a morsel. During that year I don't think I ever left the table fully satisfied, and I generally felt as though I could eat as much again as I had eaten, but when the rest of the family left I couldn't be persuaded to remain behind.

Chopping wood had been my main work during the winter. Mr. Stoddard said that in Connecticut where he had formerly lived, they could tell a man by his woodpile, and he was very particular to pile it up in good shape and furthermore he was extremely orderly in all things. His wife was even more orderly than he. I remember one time I was out playing with the boys, and I don't know how it happened, but I said, "Darn it." The old lady immediately called me up and gave me a good talking to.

It was my place to get up in the morning and start the fire in the fireplace. I always had to get up before daylight, and if I didn't happen to wake up Mr. Stoddard would awaken me. After building the fire I would sit there until the rest of the family came down, and then I would start in with the chores: feeding the horses, the sheep, and cattle, and I would chop wood until I heard the coffee mill and that sound called me to breakfast.

The first fall I was there I had a visit from Father and Mother. They came in the little wagon which had been brought over from Sweden, and as it was only about the size of a dogcart, they afforded quite a funny sight. I was very glad to see them, for up to that time I had not known of their whereabouts, but I found out all about their location and their success during the year. When they were ready to leave I went outside of the gate and started them off. I watched them drive and it made me rather sad to see them go. Suddenly the bobtailed horse, the same that was in the other runaway, took a notion he would show his speed and accordingly he started to run, dragging the little wagon after him. I was pretty scared, although I knew Father could hold almost any ordinary horse. At the end of the field a little further on there was a jungle of hazel brush and he steered the bobtail into that brush and brought the run to a sudden stop.

Sometime before I left Stoddard's, I was given permission to visit my parents. I went to LaGrange, now Orion, and found the folks living in a fairly comfortable house, and all well and happy.[2] I stayed for a few days, and then went back to the farm.

The next time I saw them was after I had left Stoddard's.

Father and Mother were in Rock Island, and were not very pleasantly located.[3] Father was troubled with diarrhea and could not work, but Mother was as tough as iron and she provided the living. When they went to Rock Island they took a cow with them, and she had strayed off during the winter and Mother was unable to find her. I went with her one day and we hunted far and near, and finally found her with a calf nearly as big as she was. That cow was the beginning of the herd we had on the farm later.

The first work I secured was for a saloonkeeper named Butcher. He had a gambling joint over the saloon and the most desperate men of the country would gather there and gamble away their money. I carried fuel for the fire and brought them anything else they wanted.

Father tried to get work, but there was nothing he could do, and after some time he persuaded me to go with him up the bluffs to chop cordwood. I think we were to get fifty cents a cord, but when we saw the tough gnarly oaks we were to cut the wood out of we gave it up as a bad job.

Djursdala Church, built in 1692. The separate belfry (*klockstapel*), to the right, is typical of many older Swedish churches. Date unknown, but probably from early in this century. (Courtesy of Nordiska Museet, Stockholm)

The interior of Djursdala Church, showing the remarkable peasant-baroque ceiling paintings Charles Hoflund recalled from his childhood. The date of this photograph is not known. The large woodstove to the right is now gone, and was not there in Hoflund's day. (Courtesy of Nordiska Museet, Stockholm)

Djursdala village, where the Hoflund family lived during the 1840s, is one of the few clustered villages of the old type still existing in Sweden after the extensive land reallocations of the nineteenth century. This photograph is from 1923, but the village had presumably changed very little since the Hoflunds left it, with the barns along the road and the dwelling houses and other outbuildings set back from it. It looks very much the same today. (Courtesy of Nordiska Museet, Stockholm)

One of the several locks on the Göta Canal at Berg, probably taken early in this century, showing the old hand-operated capstans. Here the Hoflund family, like so many other early emigrants from their region in Sweden, embarked for Gothenburg. (Courtesy of Nordiska Museet, Stockholm)

Gothenburg harbor in the mid-nineteenth century, engraving after a drawing by R. Haglund. (Courtesy of Nordiska Museet, Stockholm)

The Swedish bark *Amalia-Maria*, here shown in Bristol harbor in England, was built in 1853 and carried emigrants to America. The Hoflund family sailed on a similar vessel, the bark *Virginia*, from Gothenburg to New York in 1850. (Courtesy of the Emigrant Institute, Växjö)

The South Street quay in New York in the mid-nineteenth century. Before Castle Garden on the Battery became New York's first immigrant depot in 1855, arriving immigrants debarked directly in the city. (Courtesy of the Emigrant Institute, Växjö)

The Swedish Methodist missionary Olof Hedström's floating chapel, the Bethel Ship *John Wesley* in New York harbor, where so many early Scandinavian immigrants, including the Hoflund family, received aid and comfort. Many, again including the Hoflunds, eventually became Methodists during the earlier immigration. (Courtesy of *Swedish Pioneer Historical Quarterly*)

The first Swedish Lutheran church in Andover, Illinois, built in 1850 by Lars Paul Esbjörn, the first ordained Swedish Lutheran pastor in the American Midwest, who had arrived the year before. This church, which was later replaced by a much larger one in Andover, is now called the Jenny Lind Chapel, after the renowned Swedish singer who donated generously to its construction. It is still used for Swedish services on special occasions. (Courtesy of the Swenson Swedish Immigration Research Center, Augustana College, Rock Island, Illinois)

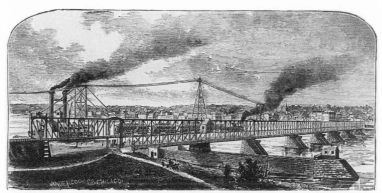

"The Great Iron Bridge of the C.R.I. & P.R.R., Crossing the Mississippi River at Davenport." Engraving from shortly after the completion of this first railroad bridge to cross the river, from Rock Island, Illinois, to Davenport, Iowa, in 1856. Charles Hoflund worked on the railroad as preparations were under way for its construction. The bridge opened the West to the expanding American railroad network. (Courtesy of the Illinois State Historical Library, Springfield)

Bank Street, Orion, Illinois, in 1875. The brick building in the middle distance was Charles Dean's store, built in 1855, two years after the town was founded. From the *Orion Times*. (Courtesy of the Illinois State Historical Library, Springfield)

Lumberjacks in the Great North Woods. This photograph was sent home to Sweden around 1900, but the scene would have been familiar enough to Charles Hoflund from an earlier day. (Courtesy of Dalarnas Museum, Falun)

Sharing snuff on the back porch of the Hoflund farmhouse near Orion, Illinois, from probably around the turn of the century. Charles Hoflund's younger brother, Gustaf Frederick is the second from the right. (Courtesy of Violet Hofflund, Rockford, Illinois)

Charles J. Hoflund in later years. (Courtesy of Grace Gregg, Hawarden, Iowa)

Christine Anderson Hoflund. (Courtesy of Grace Gregg, Hawarden, Iowa)

# 4

## The Great North Woods,

### 1851–1852

I n the meantime a young Swede came to our house and stopped for quite a little time. He was from the same part of Sweden we were and the previous winter he had worked in the pineries at Eau Claire, Wisconsin. He persuaded my folks to let me go back there with him, and he promised that I would be able to get work. I went with him, although I had just enough money to pay deck passage up to the foot of Lake Pepin, and had a balance of thirty cents left in my pocket.

We landed at Reed's Landing just below the mouth of the Chippewa River. There was one log house at that place and there we stayed overnight. One room of the building was the bunkhouse, and in the other was stored a little bit of everything of the necessities of that country, such as a few traps, red flannel shirts, Indian moccassins, a barrel of whiskey, and at one end was a small bar.

The next morning it snowed and we had about sixty or seventy miles to foot it, with packs on our shoulders, to Eau Claire. We had to cross the Chippewa river, and we were told that if we would work our way we could ride across on a flatboat. So we got our poles and poled along with the rest of them through the cold and damp. It was certainly a disagreeable task, but we managed to get over all right and started up an Indian trail toward our destination.

As we were walking along a bluff which was sparsely covered with timber, we saw an Indian buck approaching us. He was tall, straight, and erect as a pine tree. He wore buckskin breeches with little bells tied to the fringe, and carried a gun on his shoulder. This was the first Indian I had ever seen in his native haunts and it made quite an impression on me. I was somewhat apprehensive of what might happen, but John, my companion, assured me there was no danger. The Indian came right up against us, stopped in our path and said, "Bootcho nitche," which means "How do you do, friends." My pardner could understand a few words of the Indian language, so he made out that the Indian wanted to know where we were going, and he told him we were going to Eau Claire. The Indian motioned for us to move on, and for my part I was only too glad to do so.

Well, we tramped along all day and when night came I was pretty tired and awfully sore. We had good things to eat at the place where we stopped overnight, and among the good things was some wild honey. The next day we were on the home stretch for Eau Claire, and I don't remember when or in what condition we were when we arrived, but I do know that I had the very unpleasant news that there was no work for me. John had been there before and he had promise of a job if he would come back, but there was nothing for me.[1]

My chance was not very cheerful, for the boss said that there were so many seeking work. Swedes, Norwegians, Germans, and Americans came every day in squads of eight or ten to secure work, so for me the case was rather hopeless. I was put to work, however, with another man, hauling with a yoke of oxen from some low marshy ground that they couldn't get to unless it was frozen hard.

This work continued for a few days, and then I was taken sick so that I had to quit my work. I was allowed to stay in the bunkhouse. This was a long log cabin, and one end of it was used for the sleeping quarters of the mill crew. It had a fireplace and then bunks all around. These bunks were two tiers high. It was a pretty lonesome business, and to make it worse, John, the man with whom I came up there, went up to the pinery some forty or fifty miles and never said a word to me.

At one end of the bunkhouse there was a storage room in which they kept all sorts of junk. The central part, aside from being used for the entrance, was used as a sort of store where the boss kept a few things for sale such as the men would need—shirts, mittens, stockings, and the most important, I guess, was the barrel of whiskey, which the boss visited very often. His face bore the signs that he had partaken of it too freely. His name was Gage, and the company's name was Gage, Reed and Sampson. Reed and Sampson went up to the pinery or logging camp and Gage remained in charge of the mill crew.

Well, my case was rather serious and there was no doctor in the country, but after I had been there a few days by myself, someone told me to peel off the inner bark of the white oak and make a tea of it. This I did, and, with a little beef which I cooked, I managed to arrange a diet that relieved me a great deal, and in a couple of weeks I was all right again. I improved so rapidly and got so nearly well that Gage came in one day and said, "If you will cook for the mill crew and the men around the place I will give you fourteen dollars a month."

That was, of all things, the last [thing] I would have chosen to do. I would have been willing to do anything but that, but as it was I had no choice in the matter, and so I had to tell him I would try, though I did not know how to mix a batter of pancakes. The only thing that I knew I could do was to fry pork, potatoes, and things of that sort, but I had never even done that. The company had recently built a frame house where the cooking was done, and it also served as the dining room. This was the only frame house in Eau Claire at that time.

Well, I went at the cooking determined to do the best that I could. It meant, however, for the first weeks, nearly twenty-four hours a day work for me. I didn't know how to go at anything in the right way, consequently it took me night and day to find out the why and wherefore of things. The worst feature of it was I didn't know how to make a loaf of bread. Besides the stove was very small and the house stood in a clump of pine trees, so that some days there was no draft at all. It smoked me out, but of course I had to keep the fire going night and day at times.

After I had worked for a few days, chopping my own wood, and doing the work myself, a Mr. Toby, who was a baker by trade, but who was working in the mill at the time, came to me and said that he would show me how to bake bread. He did, and this was a great boon to me as I had no trouble from that source again. From that time on everybody complimented me on my bread, and that helped me not a little. The worst trouble I had was with that miserable stove, but I pegged away at it though it took me, as I have said, night and day.

After a week or two I got so completely fagged out, not having had any sleep, that I was afraid to go to bed for fear I would not be able to get up in time, and I was afraid of that man Gage, who was drunk half of the time and very mean-tempered. I begged a young Norwegian, who worked in the mill, to awaken me in the mornings at a certain time. The mill was quite a little distance up the Eau Claire River, but as he had to walk that distance and pass right by our house, he promised that he would awaken me. But he had a time getting me out. I remember one time especially, he hauled me out of the bunk onto the ground floor and I went to sleep there. Finding that this means of arousing me would not do, he pulled me outside into a snow drift, and that, of course, braced me up a little for that morning at least.

There was nothing much to cook as we did not have potatoes or butter, but we did have rice, tea, pork, and molasses (blackjack) [blackstrap?]. It was quite a task to draw this molasses in cold weather. Gage had the barrel in a dug-out cellar that was quite a ways from the house. I did not have time for the molasses to be drawn and so I left the measure and would go back in a short time and get it. But twice it happened that I put in the measure in the evening and forgot it and the molasses kept running all night. I was scared for fear the old man would find it out, and I did not know what he would do with me. I guess I felt as though he would hustle me over the bluff into the river. It so happened that the floor of this cellar was covered with sand, so I went out and found a branch and took it into the cellar, stuck it into the molasses, wound it around until it was as big as a bee hive, threw it on my shoulder and went over to the bluff and gave it a hoist. That was the way I got out of that scrape. This happened twice and the old man, fortunately, never found it out. My conscience bothered me quite a bit, but I thought it was the only and the best thing that I could very well do. When roasting coffee I would sometimes get it burned, and the coffee went the same route the molasses did.

I was afraid all the time I would hear someone make remarks about my cooking, but I heard no complaints as time went on. In addition to the crew I cooked for, I had to provide for passengers who came up on the stage line, going to St. Paul and to the West. The nearest town west was Black River Falls, and Eau Claire was the next station, and of course the team and the passengers had to be fed. Sometimes they would come in the night, and I would have to get up and prepare a meal for them. There were generally some ladies along, and I felt pretty funny and out of place. I could cook for men, but when it came to mixing up with ladies I would rather have been some other place. I remember one time I was busy in the kitchen and the stage passengers were in the dining room talking, and I could hear what they said. One lady spoke up: "This cook seems to be clean. The one at Black River was awfully dirty." It just happened that I had on a nice clean blouse which I had washed out in the morning. This was very fortunate for my reputation.

During the early part of the winter after the Chippewa had frozen over, the boss went down the Mississippi River to buy provisions. Among the things he brought back was some dressed hog, which was laid in the storehouse and, of course, froze as solid as ice. I knew that I would not be able to slice off any meat, so I found a broadax and with that I chopped off the slices as I needed them. I would chop off an armful of these slices and cook them, and at the end of the meal they would be all eaten.

Towards the latter end of the winter the men began to come down from the pineries by twos and threes, and I was kept on the jump feeding them, for they were as hungry as bears, and they made quick work of our single barrel of flour. Then too, the sawyers and mill crew wanted lunch at midnight, for at that time they had a shift. I didn't get their lunch for them at midnight and this made them pretty ugly and mean, and all this put me in a very unpleasant state of affairs for a time.

One day, I think early in March, a German came down from the timber and said he was bound for Stillwater, Minnesota. He assured me I could get twenty dollars a month in Stillwater, and so I decided to go with him.

The next day we started for Stillwater, which was a distance of ninety or one hundred miles. My companion had a satchel and I had a little bundle. I don't know what was in it, but it wasn't much, I can assure you. We couldn't get a cent of money for our winter's work and when we had insisted, Gage flew into a rage and said that he had to borrow what money had been paid out to the men and he couldn't go in any deeper for us. However, he gave us a note for the full amounts and with that we had to be satisfied.[2]

In leaving camp we were very thoughtless in not taking a particle of food with us, thinking we could make Menomonie, which was eighteen miles from Eau Claire, by noon. Well, we didn't make connections for the very good reason that we found the water in Mud Creek had risen above its banks, making it impossible for us to ford it. The weather had been mild for a few days and the snow had melted, and this, of course, raised the stream and overflowed the bottoms. We reached this creek about noon and as it was about eight miles from Menomonie we were stranded there on the prairie.

We went up and down the creek for miles trying to find some place to cross, but it was all to no purpose. In the meantime it began to get cloudy and colder, and the feeling of storm was in the air. Of course we saw that our chances of surviving that night on the open prairie were very slim, especially if a blizzard should set in. We at last came to a thicket of undergrowth, and here, amid the prickly ash and other small timber, the Indians had left a wigwam of poles. We thought probably we would be able to fix these together in some way so that we could ford the stream. We worked for a time on this plan, but when we pushed our craft into the current it was swept away like so much chaff.

On the other side of the flood we could see a shamrock swamp some distance back, and we thought if we could only make that we would have some protection from the bitter cold north wind.[3] In following down the creek some distance we found a birch tree near the bank that had been blown down. We tried to move it, but found it was frozen fast. But my pardner, John, had three matches and with two of these we built a fire and burnt the tree loose. We finally succeeded in throwing the tree across to the other bank onto the mound that had not been submerged by the water. After quite a struggle we succeeded in getting the tree into position, and with the poles from the wigwam to steady ourselves with, we ventured on this temporary bridge. We got across safe and sound but a little chilly, I will admit.

The snow had fallen for some time and had obliterated any traces of the road. We set out for the shamrock swamp we had seen, and arrived there just as it was getting dark. There was a great deal of very deep snow in this swamp and the question now was — how were we to make a fire with that one match? Our lives depended upon that match. We found an old log, scraped the snow away, cleared the log off, and then hunted among the trees for some dry moss with which to kindle our fire. It was quite a while before we were ready to risk that match, but finally John got a quilt out of his satchel and we wrapped that around us and with its shelter we managed to start a fire. Then we found dry limbs and other fuel, and with this we managed to keep it going all night. It was very cold, but with the quilt over our backs and the fire to help out we were able to keep from freezing.

It was a long and dreary night we spent, and not having had anything to eat since morning made it no better. We were some distance from the road, in fact, we were very much in doubt as to whether we would be able to find the road or not, but when morning dawned we located it all right and started on the last lap for Menomonie.

A few miles from our destination we came to a small hut where the mill company had a crew of men at work clearing and improving a farm. I found, however, upon reaching there that I had no appetite, for while carrying my bundle over my shoulder a gap had been made between my glove and coat, and my wrist was frozen. When I was near the stove, this began to swell, and took away any hunger I might have had. We reached Menomonie late at noon. The mill hands had just finished dinner and had gone to their work. But we were given a lunch, and when I asked the price of our dinner the cook said thirty cents would cover both meals all right. I happened to have the same thirty cents I had taken with me up to Eau Claire and I handed that to her. If she had demanded thirty-one cents we would have been up against it.

Now the question was whether or not to proceed to the next station that afternoon. We pondered quite a while on what to do and at last decided to start out. The nearest stop was a camp in the timber where three or four men were making shingles. We arrived there sometime after dark and the men were about ready to go to bunk. We asked if we could put up for the night, and we told them frankly that we had no money. They said they were not there for that kind of people, for everything they had cost money, and had to be freighted a long distance. So John opened his satchel and found an oil-cloth and they agreed to take us in for that. They gave us something to eat, and we were fixed all right, although our beds were on the ground.

The next place where there was any habitation was on the Elk River. Here the stage line had put up a house for the accommodation of passengers and for a change of horses. We got there just at noon and asked for dinner. John got out a white shirt from his ever-ready satchel and for that we received our noonday meal. From there we went to a farmhouse, I don't remember how far distant, and asked permission to stay overnight, but we didn't say we were broke. The next morning after breakfast when we asked the bill, the man of the house told us two dollars. I told him we didn't have two cents, and he became quite abusive to us.

"Well," I said, "we will pay you the first money we make."

"Oh, yes," he said, "I know all about that kind of a story."

"I have a note here," I said, "and I will give you that for security until you get the money, but then I want you to promise you will send the note to the post office that I will designate in the letter that contains the money." He agreed to these terms, and we again took to the road with one more difficulty safely passed.

We now went straight through to Stillwater without stopping.[4] We arrived there late in the afternoon, and before we had supper we hired out to a man, a Frenchman by the name of Big Joe, who was running rafts down the Mississippi River. While in Stillwater we boarded at the residence of a Mr. Aull. I told him of the incident of the note, and he forthwith pulled a few dollars out of his pocket and handed them to me. I wrote the letter at once telling the farmer to send the notes to the postmaster at Will River.

One fine morning that spring we were ordered to take the boats up the St. Croix River to Taylors Falls, about eighteen or twenty miles distant. Another man and myself took one boat, while Jonas Westerland and a pardner took the other boat.[5] It was a fine morning when we started out on the lake, I was in the pink of health and feeling fine. So I put in my best licks and pulled steadily all day with only a short rest occasionally to get a drink. We reached Taylors Falls just as the men were eating supper. When I stepped out of the boat I found that I was so stiff I could scarcely move and I didn't feel the need of anything to eat. I was ashamed to show anyone the pitiable condition I was in, so I went up behind a big cottonwood tree and leaning my back against it I slid down to the ground and crawled into my tent. It is easy to imagine what shape I was in the next morning. When I got up and commenced to move the pain was so unendurable that the tears streamed from my eyes.

The work for that day was to take a flatboat across a river and go into the bluffs and cut ironwood poles, carry them to the bluffs, and pitch them down into the river bottoms. After we had poles enough, the rafting commenced. The lots were placed side by side in strings of eight or ten logs wide and two hundred feet long. The poles would be placed across the logs, a hole bored in each side of the pole and straps of tough wood of the proper length were forced into these holes to make a bow over the pole. Plugs were then driven in to hold these straps in their places. This work took considerable time, and, I believe, we had eighteen or twenty strings of these logs to a raft.

We had very high water that spring in the St. Croix River, and one night as I was sleeping in my tent I thought I felt something wet at my feet. I pulled them up and after a while they felt wet again. Several others woke up with the same experience and when we looked around we found the water on the river bottom creeping around us, and our boots and trappings were floating in the tents.

We finally were ready to start on the raft from Stillwater, and I think we commenced the journey one Sunday. I remember that afternoon two young Swedes came aboard the raft and wanted work. When they went to the oars to see what they could do, they were unable to hold them properly, and as the pilot did not want that kind of men, they were set ashore. They were strangers to me and I probably would have forgotten all about the incident if one of these young men had not married my wife's oldest sister, and he remembered seeing me on that raft. In telling the folks about it, he said there was a young

Swedish lad on board who did not seem to have any trouble at all in managing the oars to the satisfaction of the pilot.

Well, we were now on our way to St. Louis, the destination of the rafts. Our pilot was a Frenchman, and we called him French Joe. He was a fine violinist and he would play quite often in the evenings, until the bluffs would reecho with the strains arising from the raft. All the time aboard the logs wasn't spent in dreariness, for we had a good deal of leisure time for fun. To me the scenery was very fascinating, especially after we got out into the Mississippi River.

We floated into the Mississippi River at Point Prescott, Wisconsin, at the foot of Lake St. Croix. From there we had about eighteen miles to Lake Pepin and in going that distance we passed through Red Wing, Minnesota. It was but an Indian village at that time. There were a great many wigwams, and we could see little patches of corn back in the bluffs. When we reached Lake Pepin we joined the rafts together and some of the men were sent out with a boat and anchor, so we towed the boat by hand. There were about twenty men on each raft, and, as we were anxious to get the logs across the lake while the weather was good, we moved along at a pretty good rate of speed.

At about the middle of the lake was a high mountain or bluff called Lover's Leap. There was a story in connection with this of an Indian warrior who wanted to marry a certain Indian maid against her wishes. He obtained the permission of her parents and came for her. But she, in order to escape, ran out on the highest point of the mountain and threw herself down. The story was romantic and we were all interested in the peak. A number of us took a boat, went ashore, and climbed the bluff.

From the time we left Stillwater until we got to St. Louis we did not have more than three nights of sleep. I don't remember how long the trip lasted, but it must have been twenty or thirty days. One day as we were nearing Dubuque, Iowa, a very strong wind came up and we had hard work keeping the raft in the channel. We had to be at the oars for hours at a time, and it was a terrible strain on me. Well, after one of those pulls, my chum, Jonas Westerland, noticed some lumps on my feet and he said,

"What's that you have on your leg?"

"I don't know what it is. I never saw it before."

"Well," he said, "that is something serious."

He was some years older than I and seemingly knew what was the matter, but I had not the least idea and so I told him I thought it would soon be all right again. He told me that some day I would know better, and I have suffered more or less all the days of my life as a result of that strain on my feet. Most of the men had, before this, fixed their oars so they would not work so hard but I didn't seem to have any trouble with mine, and then, too, it always looked as though a person wanted to slight his work when the oar was adjusted to work easier, for it didn't accomplish quite the same amount of work as before. But I have had plenty of time to regret that I let my pride get the better of my good judgment.

At different times I went down on four log rafts. One was sawed lumber and the others were logs. Twice I went to St. Louis and once to Muscatine, Iowa, and once to Galena, Illinois. The time this accident happened to me we had an old steamboat pilot and he invariably tried to follow the steamboat channel which made harder work for us. On the trip from Stillwater to St. Louis we did not tie up more than three nights, and, I believe, it took nearly a month to make the trip.

Having to be up night and day made me terribly sleepy and I remember one time while we were having a short rest I laid down and immediately went to sleep. The men didn't wake me and I had several hours of good solid sleep. While going down the Mississippi we had a chance to see some very fine scenery. Sometimes looking ahead you would think there was no outlet for the river, as the islands obstructed the course. We had to be very careful in these places for there was always danger of having the raft go aground.

When we reached a point about twenty miles from St. Louis, where the Missouri empties into the Mississippi, we were afforded a queer sight. For miles past the mouth of the Missouri there would be spots where the Missouri water would boil up with its clay mixtures, and other places where only the clear water of the Mississippi could be seen. But when we reached St. Louis it was all muddy, and the current was much swifter than before; so the question arose whether we would have to divide the raft and run half at a time or try and tie up the whole at once. It was finally decided to attempt the latter and we snubbed her up all right.

We were in St. Louis for a few days and while there I visited my first theatre. I thought the scenery was all there was to it and did not want to stay for the rest, but Jonas Westerland persuaded me to get my money's worth.

# 5

## Making Ends Meet,

### 1852–1855

From St. Louis I took a steamboat to Rock Island and from there I hoofed it home, a distance of twenty miles. When nearing home I met my brother Sander [Alexander] and a cousin of mine. They had made up their minds they were going to meet me, but as I had not written when I would be home, it was a peculiar coincidence.

When I arrived at home I did not have much to show for the time I had been away. I only had the note I had received at Eau Claire and then I had been paid for the time I worked on the raft. I remember that Father was sorely in need of money and I was sorry that I did not have more to give him.

He had just entered eighty acres of government land at a dollar and twenty-five cents per acre. Father and a Mr. Samuelson had gone up to the land office in Cambridge to enter a quarter of a section of land apiece. They could not speak English or make themselves understood, so they got my sister to interpret for them, but she was so bashful they couldn't get her to speak for them, and so in assigning the land they were given a quarter section between them instead of a quarter section each as they wanted. On the whole, however, it was just as well for Father that he did not get but the eighty, for it was quite a task to pay for that.

Now it would be possible for Mother to have a home, for that was something both she and Father had looked forward to very eagerly. I remember her saying many times that if she had a home, were it ever so humble, she would be happy and contented. The men went to work as soon as they could to improve the place and to build the house. Father worked in the timber west of the place to get wood for the framework.

As soon as we received a little money, I hired a team and went down to Moline to buy lumber. I bought some six-inch siding, and since they did not, at that time, have planed siding, I bought the rough siding. This was in the fall of the year and it was very cold and the siding froze. Of course, we wanted to economize and make the lumber go as far as we could, so we didn't lap it over as far as we should have done, and when it dried, there were large cracks left in the sides of the house. For flooring I bought a lot of maple wood which I picked out of a scrap heap. It was warped and twisted out of shape, and it was very hard to do anything with it. In laying this we did not use any joist, but father hewed off some logs and used them instead.

Well, this was the kind of a house we had the first winter, and judging from the way the snow blew in, I think it must have closely resembled a sieve. In this same house my parents lived until their death, although in a few years they were able to build a better addition to the old shack.[1] Mother was always happy in this home, and although she worked continually from morn till night, she never had a word of complaint, and sometimes I believe we would have starved if it had not been for her energetic work.

In the early fifties, in that part of the country where we were located, it was almost impossible to get work, and if you were fortunate to find a job for a day or two the wages were very low, and often you had to take it out in groceries and supplies. So we were not troubled with any serious notion of accumulating a fortune. The question with us was — how were we going to make a living?

In our neighborhood there was but one man who could afford to hire help. This was Mahlon B. Lloyd. He had what was considered in those days a large farm and he was quite a help to newcomers. He would hire the women to weed and hoe corn for him, but there was not always work for the men, so they would shoulder a pack and strike out for something to do. Often we went sixty or seventy miles on foot, a bundle on our backs, nothing in our pockets, and not knowing what would be the result of our searches.

I am not sure what I did nor where I worked during the next summer, but during the fall another Swede and I went down to Rock Island and found work in the stone quarry. The Rock Island Railroad was getting out stone for a bridge across the Rock River. After leaving here on our way home we went in bathing at the mouth of the Green River, and after I arrived home I was taken sick with the fever and ague.[2] For a time I was in a pretty serious condition, and it was sometime before I improved very greatly. I think it is likely that I stayed at home the following winter and worked at anything I could find to do.

The next summer I went up to Stillwater, Minnesota, and there I worked around at odd jobs. Some of the time I assisted a plasterer, hauled sand and lime, and mixed the mortar. I also worked in a sawmill as a night watchman. I succeeded in saving up quite a little money, but even then I was not very flush when I got home. I worked my way down on a raft to Muscatine, Iowa, in order to save railroad fare. I arrived at home finally, and, I believe, the folks were living on their eighty-acre farm. Father had managed to have fifteen or twenty acres broken in and in that he had planted sod corn and had secured a pretty good crop. He sold one hundred bushels to

Mr. Lloyd and for it he got twenty-five cents a bushel, and he thought that was the easiest money he had ever made.

About this time they were working on the Chicago, Burlington, and Quincy [Railroad], doing some grading work between Galva and Galesburg. I went out there near a place called Altona, which was about twenty miles from home. I found work here, but the wages were only a dollar a day, and, I believe, we had to pay for our board out of that. I boarded with a Swede family and worked on the road until about Christmas, when the ground froze so hard that we could not possibly do any grade work.[3] When we received our pay and were ready to go to our respective homes, quite a heavy snowstorm came up and we were forced to wade for twenty miles through the deep drifts.

Well, that winter we were busy getting out rails and materials for fencing. We had no horses or oxen, but we hired a young fellow who had a yoke, and we exchanged work with him in payment. In this way we cut enough poles to fence twenty acres. I had the job of planting trees in Father's orchard during the winter. They were the first trees in the neighborhood, and I carried them from my aunt's farm up near Orion. They were cottonwood trees, and not very small, so I was pretty tired when I reached home.

The next spring Father took a notion that he would go with me to Minnesota, in order to make a little money, so we started out with no money and only a small supply of provisions. We had friends by the name of Nelson in Rock Island from whom we thought we could borrow a little money with which to pay our steamboat fare. We knew they were pretty well fixed and we were quite well acquainted with them, but when we approached them for money, we found they were not the class of people who helped others, and we were refused the money. We were stranded there on our way to Minnesota, but we kept after the Nelsons until we at last secured our deck passage to St. Paul. After we had paid our fares on the boat, we were entirely broke and had nothing with which to buy a morsel of bread.

We went aboard a steamer at Rock Island in the evening, and in crossing the river to Davenport, Father and I were walking back and forth on the deck. It was dark and we did not see a hatch in the middle part of the boat, and Father stepped into it and hurt himself quite painfully, but not seriously. I think it took us about three days to go from Rock Island to St. Paul on the boat, and how we managed to live is more than I can say, but I imagine the boat crew saw the predicament we were in and gave us something to eat now and then.

When we arrived at St. Paul it was so late we would not make Stillwater that day, so we stayed over there with a Swede family and of course left them that much poorer for our visit. Father, on his deathbed, mentioned this family and said that he wished I could find some way in which to pay them back for their kindness. I told him I was unable to find them as I did not even know their names, and as he had given away a good many meals he would not need to have any scruples about that, so he agreed to let the matter rest.

In the morning we started for Stillwater, which was eighteen miles distant. I had gone over the road once before so we had no trouble in finding the way. When we got to Stillwater we went to a boarding house kept by a Dr. Ahl [or Aull], where I had been before and was somewhat acquainted.

We found, to our sorrow, that there was no work to be had. At that time the town of Stillwater was improving some of its streets and Father and I and two other men took a contract to cut a piece of road through some solid rock on a sidehill. After working a couple of days without the proper kind of tools, we decided that we could not go through with the job, so we quit.

As luck would have it a farmer came in town the following day and wanted someone to go onto the farm with him for the summer. Right then and there I hired out to him for twenty dollars a month, and got a good home with a good family and work for all summer.

My employer was a Scotchman who had come from Michigan. His wife had been a schoolteacher and she was the first person, as I recollect, who tried to teach me to read.[4] I learned rapidly so that I could read very soon. Every Saturday I took a trip down to Stillwater to see Father. I remember one day I went down there and upon inquiry I found that Father had gone to the lakeshore. I immediately started out to find him. Along this shore there was a projecting ledge of rock about ten feet high, beneath which were huge boulders sticking out of the water. I followed that ledge and after walking some distance I saw a person below the ledge on a rock that projected out of the water, and upon closer observation found that the person was Father. He had taken off his overalls and was standing in his shirt washing them. I remember that it aroused me not a little to see my own Father washing his overalls and putting them on wet.

After I had been on the farm for some time, Father was taken sick and was, for a time, unable to do anything. After he commenced to get better, he became acquainted with an old mason, a man who took jobs excavating basements, digging cellars, and so forth. When Father got so that he could work, he gave him a job digging out a cellar. I think he worked for this man, off and on, long enough to pay his board and as a result he was a little encouraged. Things went on much the same way until towards fall.

On Saturday I went down as usual to see Father and found that he had taken passage for home. I felt very much disappointed in his leaving without giving me any knowledge of his intentions. I found later that, on the very night of his arrival home, a peddler came to his home and asked lodging and Father of course gave it to him. It so happened that that night a prairie fire came up, and had it not been for the presence of the peddler and his help, the house would have been burned. As it was, all of the outbuildings were destroyed and our home narrowly escaped. It seemed, therefore, that Providence had a hand in his going home when he did.

I worked for this farmer until fall, helping him dig potatoes, put up his hay, and so forth. The last work, as I remember, was cutting hay. The hay there did not grow evenly like it does in Iowa or Illinois, but the best was to be found along the shores of little ponds, which were quite numerous throughout the country. The only thing that took my mind away from the monotony of the work was the flocks of pigeons that were flying around so thick that they would cast a shadow before the sun like a cloud.

After I had received my pay for the summer's work, I went to Stillwater and looked around for a job whereby I could earn my way down on a raft so as to make a little extra money instead of paying out for steamboat fare. I found a raft of sawed lumber that was to be taken down to Moline, Illinois, and I went on that and had a very pleasant trip. This was the only raft of sawed lumber that I ever rode on, and it proved to be much nicer than logs.

When I got home I had quite a little money, not as much as Vanderbilt, but I felt pretty good about the little sum that I had accumulated.[5] The folks and my sister had traded on credit and had some pretty heavy bills to meet and some of my money went to pay them off. In fact, I never thought of my own interests when it was a question of the money I had earned, but I always gave it to help the folks out of their hard straits.

The winter following, which was the winter of 1853 and

1854, I stayed at home and helped Father haul wood and rails and during this time I think I spent about three weeks in school. At that time we had no schoolhouse in our district, but they hired a room from a family who had moved down into the lower part of the house, which was really a dugout, and who, in order to make a few dollars, had rented their upper rooms to the district. The school was held in that room by a retired Presbyterian preacher, who passed as a teacher.

In the spring of 1854, I went to work for a farmer near Rock Island. Jim Samuelson was working there, and through him I secured employment. During that summer the first train entered Rock Island, and upon that occasion they had quite a big celebration.[6] All of the people for miles around went down to the city for the festivities. I worked at this place for a few months, and when I finally quit, it was because of the persuasion of a man who was working in a livery stable in Rock Island. I secured a job with him, but I did not like the work, although there were many times when it was not so disagreeable. John Dietricht, from whom I obtained this job, now lives in Geneseo and is one of the leading merchants of that town.

The latter part of that summer I went to Augusta, Hancock County, Illinois, to work on the Chicago, Burlington, and Quincy Railroad. There were a great many Swedes who went down there at the same time and I became intimate with several of them. At that time they were grading the road and all that were in my company went to work on the grade, shoveling. But I hired out to a German who was digging the railroad well, and for this work I got a little better pay than the rest of the men. I boarded at the home of a farmer by the name of Austin.

We worked at that well for a considerable length of time, a couple of months at least. When finished it was thirteen feet in diameter. We had to dig through very tough material, which made progress exceedingly slow. The season was uncommonly dry, so nearly every well was empty and the creeks were dried up, and there was a great need for water. When we got down about forty feet, and had worked there for quite a while, the engineer came and talked with our boss, and he said if we could not get water in ten feet or so he would change the locality. In the meantime, he went to Quincy and had some augers fixed so as to be able to reach down ten or fifteen feet deeper. He had even used lightning rods to probe, but the soil was so hard that the rods bent and we were forced to get the auger.

One sultry, hot day another man and I were working down in the well filling the buckets, and the boss and another man were turning the windlass. As it was so sultry and warm, my German pardner spoke up all of a sudden and said:

"I am going up. I am all wet and this heat makes me sick."

He hollered, "Hist," and they hoisted him up, and then something came over me just as naturally as if someone had whispered in my ear, "You go up too." I had never gone up before to change shirts or for any other reason, although the German would go up quite frequently. But this came over me in such a convincing way that I was forced to yield. They, therefore, hoisted me up also, and as soon as I got out I commenced to pull off my shirt. As it was wet it stuck a little and it took me sometime to get it off, but before I did get it laid aside the well had caved in twenty feet, and to say that I was thankful for being above ground would be putting it mildly.

Now the question with the engineer was — would we go on and clean out the well or not? He finally decided to keep on in the same place. We had to use curbing all the way up, and it took some time to clear away this cave-in, but we finally got it out, and after it was cleared we used a two-inch auger testing for water. Well, we probed all over the floor of the well but without result. Now we had bored in three places at different angles and were about to give it up as a bad job when another Swede fellow and I decided to bore another hole in one corner of the well, and when we got within two or three inches of the floor of the well, the auger dropped down and the water commenced to force up through the hole in the floor. The men at once went to work and made an oaken plug and with it stopped the hole. The news of this water find created as much excitement as though we had struck a vein of gold.

When we got everything fixed as we thought it ought to be, we came up out of the well and went home. Early Sunday morning, however, we went down there to see how things stood. We found that the well had filled up to within about eight feet of the top. The people had hauled out watering troughs and had a pump in so that the stock could be watered. The whole neighborhood could have been watered.

The winter following I stayed at home, and I do not remember anything of special importance that happened that winter. We had a big blizzard about the 21st of January [1855] and it was said to be the worst that ever struck the country. I had quite a time trying to keep the cattle at home, and finally, in spite of my efforts, they did stray off into the field of a neighbor. I succeeded in getting them nearly home, when they again bolted and this time made for a protected slough where I was forced to leave them.

I remember one day about two months later when the snow was melting, I noticed a black spot on what was left of a huge drift near the farmhouse, and upon investigation, I found a chicken which was still alive, but with its feet frozen to the ground. It undoubtedly had been snowed under in the January blizzard and had managed to live until March.

# 6

## Loggers, Indians, and Tight Money, 1855–1856

In the spring following, 1855, I went up to Stillwater, Minnesota, for the last time. I met Jonas Westerland again and he got me a job in a sawmill south of Stillwater. I worked there with him at odd jobs throughout the summer. Part of the time I was a tail-sawyer, part of the time I piled lumber, and part of the time I hauled logs to the mill from Lake St. Croix.

One incident while I was here in the mill is well worth relating, for it made an impression on me that lasted all through my life. It occurred while I was hauling in logs for the mill. The work required that the mill be kept running night and day, so I worked half of the day and half of the night. The logs were held in a boom, and in the daytime I generally managed to have enough logs on hand so I would not have to go out on the boom at night and get them. This night, however, a thunderstorm came up and with it a very strong wind which blew from the shore. It carried the logs out to the farther end of the boom, and as I had no boat, the only way I could get to them was to climb on a log and ride out.

The night was pitch dark, and it was pretty risky business, but I got out all right, and was immediately confronted with the more perplexing question of how to get back with more than one log. I felt around with my pike pole and got three or four logs together. I then mounted the hindmost log and endeavored to scull the others ahead of me against the wind. As I could not touch bottom and could not ride very well, I tried riding two logs at once with the result that I was dropped into the water, an experience which any old-timer at log-riding could have foretold. Well, there I was, all alone in the dark. It was impossible to make myself heard above the din of the mill and I couldn't swim a stroke. The first thing I touched upon coming to the surface was the pike pole and that probably saved my life. Now, how was I to board the log again? I knew I could not get over the sides, for I had tried it myself and had seen others try it, so I worked my way around to the end and succeeded, after quite an effort, in climbing onto the timber.

After I quit the mill I went up to Stillwater, and I made up my mind to take a vacation of two or three weeks, as I had not been feeling very well of late. I looked up a boarding place with a German family, where I expected to stay while idle. But one day while out walking with another Swede, we met a Mr. Schulenberg, who owned a mill a few miles up the lake. He wanted to know if we were looking for work and we told him we would work if there was a good opportunity. Well he said if we could ride logs and handle a boom he would give us a job at the mouth of the St. Croix River. He told us that he had a boom across the river in order to catch the logs and lead them up to his mill, but the steamboats which sometimes passed through there in the night sometimes ran down the boom and made trouble. He needed someone to open the boom for any boats that happened along, and so he offered us two dollars a day and our board and lodging. We were given permission to get lumber at the mill and build us a little shanty.

We worked here for ten days and the twenty dollars I received was the easiest money I ever earned in my life. We really had nothing to do and slept day and night. Twice a boat came up, ran against the boom, and rang the bells and nearly frightened us to death. After we were through with this work we hired out to a lumber company and went about sixty-five miles up the Wood River [in Wisconsin]. I hired out as a cook at thirty dollars a month, and John, my pardner, hired out as an ordinary chopper at twenty dollars a month.

We made the trip to Wood River by the ox-team route, and it took us two or three days to get there with the two or three yoke of oxen we had. When we arrived in the pinery the snow was deep, and it was a great strain on me, worrying about rolling out before daybreak, scraping away the snow and kindling the fire out in the open air.

The first thing the men did was to build a cabin. It was about twenty-eight feet square and two [?] feet high. There was a door at the gable end and a table at the other, but not a window in the building. Through the center from one gable to the other we laid down a floor of split logs. I imagine this floor was fourteen or fifteen feet wide, and in the center of it we made a fireplace by putting dirt on the logs. At one end of the fireplace we erected a crane on which to swing the kettles and cooking utensils. On the sides of the fireplace the men built some benches and back of these were our bedding grounds. We had filled in this place with leaves, straw, and blankets, so we were pretty comfortably fixed.

I was very glad when we got into the new building, so that I could make good bread. The boss told me I should sleep alongside of him so we could awaken each other, for there wasn't a single watch or timepiece among the whole crew of fourteen or fifteen men. The result was that I would some-times prepare breakfast at one or two o'clock in the morning. I would call the men to breakfast, but they objected to the early hour and so would go back to sleep, and so consequently I would have to get the second meal. But after a while I regulated my rising by the position of a star above a certain pine tree, and that made things easier. I don't remember that I started the men late once during the whole of that winter. But it kept me pretty busy, for I wasn't very well trained in the business and I had to carry all of my own water, chop my own wood, and was bothered a great deal by the Indians who came straggling through the camp occasionally.

I became quite intimate with one and from him I learned a number of Indian expressions. The squaws caused me the most trouble. They would steal anything they could lay their hands on, even the soap, and I kept a pretty close watch on them when they were around. The bucks never bothered me in that way. They would often come with a part of venison or a string of fish and would ask to trade it for flour or meal, and I took it upon myself to make the trade and in that way we got a little fresh meat and a change of grub.

When I got venison I would put it into the Dutch oven, dig a place in the ashes, and heap it over with hot coals and leave it that way all night. In the morning when I took it up it would be so tender it would fall to pieces, and when the men got ahold of it, the whole business vanished like mist before the sun. One morning the men went out and killed nineteen pheasants, and I cooked them in the same way.

It was very cold in that part of Wisconsin, which was not far from Lake Superior, but I was very comfortable and didn't hear any complaint on the part of the men. I mentioned the fact that the Indians came every week or so. There were two who came somewhat oftener than the others. One was quite a nice-appearing buck about forty years of age; the other was an older man, a homely, cross-looking rascal, and I hated to have him around. I would occasionally give the younger one a cup of coffee. In the latter part of the winter this younger, friendly

Indian came in and the first glimpse I got of him I could see that he had been sick or that something was the matter. He then showed me that his hand was wrapped up in rags and I tried to find out what was the trouble. He told me that a short time before he had gone down to Taylors Falls, and while there he and some other Indians had gone on a drunk and consequently gotten into a row. While fighting there, he was pushed into the fire, and one of his hands was severely burned. His only explanation was, "White man's firewater very bad."

The Indians had a village about three miles from our camp. One morning about sunrise, when I started down to the creek for water, I saw a couple of Indians outside of the shanty. It had been snowing and they were evidently resting themselves against the side of the building. The buck was a tall young man, and the girl was short and stoutly built. He stood there with his gun on his shoulder, and she had a roll of carpets and some cooking utensils. The bundle was about as tall as she, and so strapped that she could hang it over her shoulder. When they started to go, she knuckled down and tried to lift it, but it pulled her to the ground. She tried again, and this time succeeded in raising it, but the load was all she could possibly manage. He never touched it with his finger. That seemed to be beneath his dignity.

Towards the latter part of the winter, one day, after the men had all gone to work, quite a large company of young bucks came until they seemed to crowd the cabin full. They seemed to take possession of everything, and I couldn't hardly move. They talked among themselves in their own language and pointed at me. I couldn't afford to get scared. They washed themselves and combed their hair and after a short stay they went the same way they had come and I was glad to see them depart, for the winter before they had killed a young Swede just for the deviltry of it, and I didn't relish any of their tricks being played on me. From what I saw of the Indians up there, I made up my mind that on the whole they were fairly good people, and if treated right, would do the square thing by a person.[1]

The company for whom I worked had three camps a mile or so apart, and the bosses were three brothers. Our boss, Joe Jackson, was the youngest, next came Jack, and Bill was the oldest. Joe Jackson was a teamster and drove a logging team. That was the most responsible position in the logging camp, and it took a great deal of practice to handle a team of oxen. At one time during the winter our boss was sick for a few days, and to fill his place they picked out a man who had broken oxen in Illinois. But this change of drivers certainly made a big difference. The men had scarcely anything to do. In hauling out trees they wouldn't be cut into saw lengths, but the tree would be hauled out onto the dam and there two men would do the sawing.

You take a tree that has several log lengths in it and it would make you hustle some to get it through the timber. I would often stand by the door and watch Jackson come through the timber. There was a little rise near the cabin, and when he drove over that, the logs would raise up the sled and the oxen would scratch on the ice like cats. The house would shake, so valiantly did the oxen fight to keep their pace with their little shoes. If Jackson didn't think one of the oxen had done his duty he would unhitch and chain it to a tree and then go at it with the goad. The blood would trickle down on the snow and the poor ox would simply roar.

When the snow began to melt and we had to quit logging, I think we moved down the St. Croix River to a sort of halfway station, and here we remained until the ice was out of the river and partly out of the dam so that we could begin work. When we again went up the river there were about seventy men in the crew. There was one Norwegian in the crew who was a complete circus all by himself. He kept the crew continually amused by his singing, fighting, and wrestling. He was real good-looking and about as fine a young fellow as I ever met, although he tried pretty hard to kill himself. Each night we went into camp, and then we had all sorts of games and contests in which we tried each other's strength at jumping, wrestling, pole vaulting, and throwing handspikes. There were some real good storytellers among the bunch, and we would sit on a log around the campfire and listen to their stories or their singing until midnight.

When we reached the place where we had been logging for the winter, our camp was farther up on the river than some of the other camps. The logs here were rolled into a dam which was made to hold water enough to float the logs. They were shoved through a sluiceway made for that purpose, and then our business was to see that they did not jam in the rapids below. In some places it was possible for one log to so lodge that it would cause a jam of the whole drive, so we were required to keep a very close watch.

I will never forget that first day on the log drive. A good many had practiced and were used to log-driving, but many others had never tried the experiment before. As it was, I had received quite a little experience while working on the boom at Stillwater, so I got along fairly well. But the poor fellows who hadn't any experience took a good many duckings, and as the weather and water were quite chilly a plunge wasn't a thing to be most enjoyed, especially when most of the men did not have a change of clothes. Everything was quite exciting. As I looked down the creek as far as I could see, there were floating logs, with a man here and there all the way for some distance. Every once in a while a yell would be given that so and so had been given a ducking, and every time a person was baptized this thing was repeated. But I kept myself dry. Our efficiency was rated according to our ability to ride.

We commenced sometime in March and I think it was about the first of June when we reached the St. Croix River. When we arrived at the second camp the logs had to be thrown over a precipice near what was called Little Wood Lake. The first day we went to work here it was cold and a snowstorm came up in the afternoon. We were forced to wade into the water quite often and pry out the logs, which would get mixed in all sorts of shapes when thrown into the stream from the bluff. This was the most trying incident I had in the whole business. It seemed at first that it would be impossible to stand the cold, and if I had had any money to give I would have given the last dollar to get out of it. Three or four men did break away and go into the woods where they could build a fire. But when the rest of the crew saw it they chased them back to work again. All were interested in getting the logs down, for the men had gone to work with the understanding that if they did not get them down they wouldn't get their pay, so they determined everyone should do his part and nobody shirk. The only way it was possible to live was to work with all one's might to keep from freezing, at least that was the way I managed it.

Right on the bank of Little Wood Lake was a village of Chippewa Indians, and there I learned something of their life. I went up to the camp one day and took a survey of their wigwams. The first one we looked into was that of an Indian squaw, who, we were told, was one hundred and twenty years old. She looked more like a monkey than a human being. She said, "When I was a girl I could take hold of the tops of those logs you are now floating away, and bend them to the ground."

I remember one noon, Jackson, the boss of the middle camp, was throwing handspikes and when he was through he stuck his into the ground. A young Indian buck picked up another spike and threw it, hitting Jackson's spike and splintering it. Jackson lost his temper and slapped the Indian in the face. The Indian ran to his wigwam and started back with his rifle, but the squaws held him back. He didn't succeed in doing any shooting, but took his station near camp and kept his eye on us all afternoon. The men were, on the whole, displeased with Jackson's conduct, fearing trouble with the Indians, although the result of a fight would probably have been in our favor for we were seventy in all and young fellows waiting for some excitement.

There was an incident in the drive from the first camp down to the second camp which I will relate here. It was near quitting time, and the men were occupied with what they called "sacking up," or gathering up the tail end of the drive. Some of the logs would lodge along the shore in the shallow water, and it was necessary to roll them out into the current, and the only way to manipulate them properly was to jump on and ride them out. As we were nearing the campsite, a great many men were bunched up on the last few logs and I happened to be on an unusually large one that was partially dried or dead. I don't remember how many there were on this log, but it was piled to its full capacity.

In the crowd there was a young Frenchman whom we called Mike. He had been on several drives before and prided himself on being an expert at the business. He, naturally, started the log rolling a little and the men not wanting to be dumped into the water asked him not to turn it. But he paid no attention, and the log was soon going fast enough so that one by one the men dropped off. Some of the members of the sawmill company were watching the men, and, I think, Mike wanted to display his prowess to them, so he kept tossing one to the right and one to the left until I was the only one left. I was at one end and Mike at the other, and I made up my mind to stick to that log if it was a possibility. But I had to run with all my might in order to keep my balance, and the water fairly flew around us. The men standing on the bank would call out to me: "Stick to her." "Throw him in."

Well, when Mike found he couldn't get me off, he began to move towards my end of the log, and as he was a big man, I knew if he ever reached me he could shove me in. But the log kept him pretty busy, and just as he was coming within reach of me, he made some misstep, and away he went into the water, handspike and all. The men set up a great "Hurrah," and I felt pretty elated when I stepped onto the shore with a dry shirt.

We had four meals a day during the drive. These meals were in the form of a lunch and would be carried around to us by the cook and his attendant. It was quite a task to carry the cooking outfit along with us as we floated downstream. Sometimes they would have to move every day and again only every other day. But altogether it made a great deal of work for the cook.

I don't remember how long it took us to get the logs into the Little Wood Lake, but it took us only a short time to tow them from there to the outlet in the Wood River. Here the stream was much larger and flowed a much greater volume of water. It took us several days to get the logs from the Wood River into the St. Croix and then we had lighter work since the stream was much wider and the tendency to form jams wasn't so much.

The weather was becoming warmer and we had to fight the mosquitoes continually; they were so thick we could scarcely breathe. After the logs were safely in the St. Croix River we left them there to take care of themselves and go down without any guidance. But when we reached Taylors Falls we had to be extremely careful for the danger of jams was very great, and occasionally one would form in spite of our precautions.

After I arrived at Stillwater I hired out to work on the boom. The logs were marked the same way that cattle are branded in the West. They were marked on the land and then rolled into the water where these brands would often be submerged. They, therefore, had a certain number of men in the boom, who were familiar with these marks, to mark them on top in the water so they could be distinguished. My particular work was to catch the logs as they came floating down the river. We had long poles with steel spikes in the end and we would fasten these into the logs and pull them up to the shore. As far as we could reach, we would spike the logs and pull them up to where we stood. If the logs I had were marked with the brand for which I was looking, I would tie them up with a rope and then let them float down to where they were making a raft for the Mississippi.

We had our boarding tent on a high bluff not far from the river. The sleeping tent was long and made with bunks on each side and an aisle down the center. One morning when we awoke we noticed the tracks of a bear on the ground floor of this tent, and some of the men said they had heard a peculiar sniffing noise early in the morning. There were bears in the neighborhood, and I should judge it must have been an ideal country for them, for there were bluffs, cliffs, stone, and timber in great abundance and hardly any settlers had yet entered the country.

When I finished work on the boom I went down to Stillwater, and the first thing I did was to see Mr. Lowell and ask for my pay. He was willing to make a settlement all right, but there was no money to be had. His agreement was that he was to pay the men providing they got the logs into the Mississippi, and his excuse was that the water in the river was so low they could not be rafted. I then asked him to give me a note and he refused me that also.

Well, I was stranded. I had just received a letter from home stating that my sister Caroline had died and my parents were anxious for me to come home as soon as possible. I had hardly any money and the outlook wasn't bright for any more, so I was in a pretty bad state of affairs. When I went up to see Mr. Lowell a second time he still refused me money, but he said he would pay me with logs that bore the company's mark. I readily accepted this offer and persuaded my pardner, John, to go in with me. In a few days several others joined us in this venture, among them an old man from Maine, who had been away from home for a number of years and was very anxious to get out of the pineries with a little money. So altogether we had quite a little crew and we were soon fitted with the necessary rope, boat, and the tools of our profession.

We worked for some time getting out what we thought to be our allotted amount of logs, and then the company sent down its surveyor to see if our estimate was correct. When each one had the right number of feet they made arrangements to sell, and all except John and I sold to a firm in Hudson. But I was determined to float our logs down the Mississippi River even though the water was low, and so John and I went to rafting.

After several weeks of work our raft was completed and we started down the Lake with it. Now that we had cut loose from the shore it was necessary that we lay in a supply of food, so we went ashore and into a new town that was just starting, and here bought some crackers, cheese, and a chunk of ham. When we went back to the raft we decided we would run it through the lake as quickly as possible so as to avoid any storm which might come up and demolish it before we had it under our complete control. So we worked a good part of the night, and very early in the morning John was taken suddenly and terribly sick.

I didn't know what to do, but pulled the boat onto the raft and fixed a place for him to lie down. I was afraid he would die before morning. When morning finally dawned he was still suffering very greatly, and leaving the raft, we put out together in the boat. I had heard of a mill on the Wisconsin side near a stream call the Kinnikenick, and I made for it. When I reached the stream I had to carry John on my back, and that way I managed to get him to the mill. I asked the people there to care for him and I went back to the raft.

All of that day, the next night, and nearly all of the next day I labored to get the logs through the lake, and at last reached the mouth where I could feel the current drawing me along. Here I fastened the raft ashore and was just going up the bank when I heard someone approaching, and looking up I found it was John. He had walked about eighteen miles that day. He was very glad to see me and to see the raft so near the river.

While John and I were reconnoitering around the lake we met a man who asked us if we were the parties who were running the logs down the Mississippi River. We told him that we were, and he then offered us nine dollars a thousand for our timber. Well, we agreed to let him have them at that price and went to a lawyer's office to make up the papers. When we reached the office, Manning, the man who bought the logs, said he did not have the money for all, but he did have a note of three hundred and seventy-five dollars on a Mr. Mechum which he said he would turn over to us in part payment. I did not know either Manning or Mechum so I hesitated. But the lawyer nodded to me that it was all right and I said I would accept. John received, for his logs, a note on someone else. My agreement was that I should work for Manning in his lumberyard until I received pay for the logs. He said he would have to have a little time and he would meanwhile pay me twenty dollars a month and board for my work in the yard.

I think that I worked in this yard about a month and then I was taken with an affliction under my arm. It bothered me so much I had to quit work and I told Mr. Manning that if I could get my money I would leave. But he said since times were so hard he would have to let the payment go for a while. He told me he couldn't get any money for the lumber which he sold. In the meantime he agreed to pay my board at the hotel until I was able to get the money. So I went to the hotel with this understanding.

There I was for some time, and to make matters worse I heard that this Mr. Manning was broke. It was getting late in the season and I was afraid I would have to stay up there all winter, so I kept chasing him around wherever I could find him. I would tackle him every day and I have thought many times since that if he hadn't been of a mild temperament he would have blown me up.

Well, I remained up there week after week and payday seemed just as far off. One day the landlord came to me and told me that Mr. Mechum was going to his old home in New England for a visit. This man had a sawmill about two miles from town on the lakeshore. The landlord told me the time he expected to leave and now the question was what could I do? I believe I went to a lawyer and had the matter arranged so that he could be stopped.

Towards the latter part of the time I stayed there at the hotel, Manning came to me and said that upon such and such a day in the next week he would pay me. He warned me, however, that I should not show the notes to Mechum and he was very particular in his warning. One day as I was brooding over this matter my curiosity got the better of me and I made up my mind to go up to the mill and see Mr. Mechum. So I went up one afternoon and found him in the sawmill. He was a large middle-aged man with a prepossessing appearance.

When I told him I had a note on him, told him the circumstances of getting it, and showed it to him he flew into a
terrible rage and said: "The damned scamp, the damned
scamp. I paid that note to him, every cent of it."

He said he didn't have enough with him at the time to pay
the interest so that was still due. He told me he would bring it
that next evening and said he would pay that. The next
morning [Manning] came to the hotel. He was very excited for
he had found out I had shown the note to Mechum. I thought
he would start a fight with me, but I told him I had to do it for I
had been waiting around for it for weeks, and he had promised
to pay it every day. With Mr. Mechum going east in the near
future something had to be done. I told Mr. Mechum that
arrangements had been made to stop him if he tried to get
away without paying that note.

Well, I rather think that had a soothing effect on Manning.
At any rate, it cooled him down some. On a certain day in the
next week he promised to pay me and he told me to remain in
the hotel office and wait for him even though it was late at
night. Of course, I had hopes of pay, but I had been deceived so
often I did not rely very much on promises. To my great
surprise and delight he did come on the appointed day and said
he was ready to fix things up. But he said I would have to go
with him to see Mr. Mechum.

It was now about ten or eleven o'clock at night, but I told
him I would go with him. He had a horse and a democrat
wagon. We got in and drove up the lakeshore to Mechum's
mill. It was not a very pleasant ride for me, I must confess.
When we arrived at the mill we found that the Mechums had
all gone to bed, but Mr. Mechum answered the call at the door
and let us in. Well, he gave me the face of the note, I am not
sure whether it was three seventy-five or three eighty-five.
The amount of the logs would have been a little over four

hundred dollars, and then I had twenty dollars coming to me for the time I had worked in the lumberyard. When I asked him [Manning] for the balance, he turned on me like a tiger, but I don't remember whether he swore or not, though I didn't pursue that subject any further. He said if I knew the circumstances I would be more than thankful for what I had already gotten. "If all of my creditors fared as well as you have they would be too," he added. I was thankful and I was certainly glad that I got the matter off my mind.[2]

The next boat that came along I took for Reed's Landing. From there I went to North Pepin, but found nothing from Stone or any of the proceeds from my note. I then determined to go up to Eau Claire, and so I took the stage on the following morning. As the stage was speeding along the road we passed a man driving a team, and as I looked out I thought I recognized the driver as Stone, the man whom I let have the note, and sure enough, much to my surprise, it was he.[3] He was bound for North Pepin and I got in and rode back with him. He seemed in a quandary to know why the money had not arrived there for he said he had sent it. But he still thought it would come, although I finally made up my mind that he was a crook and had decided to keep the money for himself. I told him that I would go up to Eau Claire with him and work there for the winter.

During all this time he seemed to be endeavoring to rid himself of me, but I kept my nose on his tracks and followed him wherever he went. He appeared to be extremely busy and claimed to have a great deal of business to transact. Late one day, however, he said he was going to start for North Pepin and I told him I would go along. But as we were approaching the boat landing where we were to cross the lake, he turned to me and said he would give fourteen dollars for the note. Well, when I thought I couldn't get anything more out of him I decided to accept his offer.

That fourteen dollars with the ten I had received a year or so before from one [member] of the sawmill firm whom I happened to meet in Rock Island, was all I was paid for my first winter's work in the pineries.

# 7

# Settling Down,

## 1856–1869

Now I was indeed glad to take the boat for home. I arrived at Rock Island after an uneventful trip on the river, and from there I expected to walk home, which was a distance of about twenty miles. But I met an acquaintance in Rock Island who kindly offered me a ride. He lived in Swedona, a little way from our home, and after staying at his home for a night, I was then taken the rest of the distance the next day.[1]

On my arrival home I guess Mother was the first to see me, and she threw her arms about my neck and wept for joy. I had about four hundred dollars to the good when I reached home, and I had been advised by my kind friend, Mr. Wallerstadt, who drove me from Rock Island, to invest this sum in land. But I found the folks were owing quite heavy store debts at Orion and I felt my first duty was to help them, so I paid their bills ungrudgingly. Besides settling up several other debts of Father's, I bought a heavy wagon which cost eighty dollars, but the folks were sorely in need of it and it was money well invested. I had just enough money left, after these settlings and purchases, to buy a yoke of oxen for which I paid sixty-five dollars.

I think it was during the following winter that I had the

privilege of attending school for a short time. I went off and on for about three weeks that winter. This was in the winter of 1856 and 1857. In the evenings when I was not studying I often visited our neighbors, the Samuelsons, who lived on the same quarter section that we did. They had several boys at home and we had good times together.

I remember particularly one evening we were talking about the young people of the neighborhood, and in overhauling the names of the girls of the countryside, one of the boys said, "There is a girl living between Andover and Cambridge, and her name is Anderson."

Some way or other that name fastened itself upon me so that I made it a point to keep a lookout for that girl. This impression lasted until I finally made her acquaintance and then it was made the more forceful.

In the latter part of the winter I went down to a territory not far from Abington, near Galesburg. I took our team and the wagon I had purchased and went to work for the Chicago, Burlington, and Quincy [Railroad], hauling cordwood. This enterprise proved an entire failure. The weather and the roads were such that it was impossible to travel in an empty wagon, much less one loaded with cordwood. I at last became so discouraged, not having anything I could do, that I struck out for home. The roads were so bad that I was afraid the horses would break their legs. In places they would go up to their bellies in the mud. I came home with a little more experience, but no more money.

There is nothing of importance now to relate for a period of some years [after 1857], only the ordinary events which come to a lad assisting his father on an eighty-acre frontier farm.

In the meantime I had settled one thing, and that was the girl. One Sunday while in church I happened to take a survey of the crowd and my eyes wandered to a bunch of girls. Some of them I knew as belonging to Methodist families, and I made up my mind that my lass was among them. I was right in my conjecture, and when I had fully verified my belief, I determined that she was the girl for me.

At that time we belonged to the Lutheran church, but for some time I had attended the Methodist meetings, which were held in the schoolhouse and private homes. Besides this, I had obtained some Methodist literature written by a Mr. Fletcher, one of the leading ministers of the day. From reading and hearing I was thoroughly convinced that the Methodist doctrine was the right one for me, assisted in my conclusion, perhaps, by the presence of the girl in that church. There was a great deal of disputing going on between the different churches. You couldn't meet a neighbor without getting into some sort of a doctrinal argument with him, and anything like a change from one church to another was considered very seriously.[2]

About this time, the fall of 1858, I bought a threshing machine in partnership with a man by the name of August Peterson. We ran the machine for two seasons. Although we had no experience, we got along remarkably well, and had the name of being the best threshers in the country. One of our mottoes was always to be on time, and we would reach our destination on the day set if we had to use the night in traveling.

One time we were threshing for a Mr. Burgeson, who lived south of Andover, and they had exchanged work with some of the neighbors. Among others who were there was the father and brother of the girl I had selected as my future wife. I did not know them at the time nor did I know who they were, but some way or other I was very much impressed with everything about them — their team, harnesses, and so forth. I think that was the first time I ever saw Father Anderson and his son, Gus.

I don't remember when I first began calling on Christine
Anderson, but I do remember very distinctly the time I made
my proposal to her.[3] I went with the Andersons from church
one Sunday, as did also a young lady friend of Christine's. I
much preferred privacy that afternoon in particular, but this
girl stuck to the object of my affections like a leach or a piece
of sticking plaster. But I thought I would hit on a scheme and
take my girl out with the horse and buggy, and the other girl,
not being invited, would surely not go along. But, alas! she
climbed in too. I drove along through a woods near the farmhouse; finally, noticing some flowers growing by the roadside,
I asked this young lady to pick some for us. Well, she did and I
whipped up the horse and drove away. Before we returned I had
the promise for which I had been hoping.

On the last day of 1860 we were married at my wife's
home. Rev. A. J. Anderson, the Methodist minister performed
the ceremony. Among other friends present was the father-in-
law and mother-in-law of A. J. Anderson. It must have been a
very pleasant affair, for whenever I met A. J. Anderson's father-
in-law, he would always say that our wedding was the most
pleasant ceremony he had ever witnessed, and he predicted a
most happy journey for us together. After a short time we went
to the home of my parents, as I felt I had sort of an interest in
that place. We lived there for two years after our marriage.

In the latter part of the winter of 1863 I went over to a
neighbor, a widow lady who had a farm that cornered with
Father's, to borrow a spade. She wanted to rent me her farm,
and such a proposition just suited me. I agreed to rent her farm
for a term of four years, and in talking things over she told me
she had some cattle and some farming implements that she
wanted to dispose of. Well, the outcome of it all was that I not
only rented the place but I bought everything she had on it.

When spring came I moved down to this, the Craft place. I

worked the eighty [acres] I had rented for two years and then I rented another place adjoining. One day Mrs. Craft, the owner of the farm, came to the house and said she wanted to sell. I told her I would like to buy, but that I had no money with which to buy. She said she would sell on time if that would help me any. She wanted thirteen or fourteen dollars [per acre], I am not sure which. There was a fairly good house on the place, so it struck me that her price was cheap enough and I agreed to take the land. That was the end of the deal for a few weeks, but after some time she came down again and told me she rued the bargain. She had been told that her price was altogether too low, and I asked her if she felt that way herself. She said that she did. As long as that was the case, I told her she could have the papers back again and so I let her have the land.

Sometime in the winter of 1865 we went home to my wife's folks for a visit, and while I was there my brother-in-law told me that John Sackrison had been figuring on buying some land in Osco Township, but the party who had the sale of the land would not part with one quarter unless they could sell the two. The result was that after figuring on this he gave it up as too much of an undertaking. Finally, however, he went to my brother-in-law, A. G. Anderson and told him that if he would take one-half of the land, he, Sackrison, would buy it.

Gus told me this and then he said he refused to accept the bargain, but he said if I would go in he would buy it with me. After we had found that Sackrison had given it up altogether, we decided to go to the agent in Geneseo, Andrew Crawford, and see what kind of a deal we could make. We found that the price and terms were just as we had understood them to be, but after talking the matter over, my brother-in-law said he thought he would back out of the deal altogether, as he did not feel as though he could go into that much debt.

When I found he was determined not to take it, I decided

to take the whole of it myself, but I thought so much of Gus Anderson I didn't feel I wanted to take any advantage. Had it been any other man, I would have been too glad to have jumped in and taken the whole thing, because Gus told me he would help me break it, and I wouldn't need to pay him until I had raised enough money from my crops to pay him. I turned to Gus and said that I would buy the land all alone, and I asked him if he wouldn't go in with me. He said if he could go in that way it would be all right. So we went up and bought the land. We bought three hundred and twenty acres at fourteen dollars an acre.[4]

In the spring of 1865 my brother-in-law A. G. Anderson drove down to Rock Island with our team and bought three thousand feet of lumber. He went in the morning and came home late that night. In order to get the lumber where I wanted to build he had to go through a slough, which was impossible at that place, and in order to get the lumber on the north side of the slough we would have to go around it, and so I decided to unload our lumber on the south side and build our little shack there.

The three thousand feet of lumber we purchased built the whole house — frame, roof, sides, and floors, and we had a few boards left over. We had no flooring, so we used just common boards, and my wife remarked several times that it was a very easy matter to keep the floor clean, as the water would run through the cracks and she had no trouble with the mopping. In that house we lived over sixteen years, though I made some improvements later on and built an addition.

As I look back now, I cannot see how it was possible for my wife to get along with the work that she had to do. She always had a number of men around to cook for, and she had two children, Eddie and Julia.[5] She managed to get along so well that I never heard a complaint. Everyone left her table satisfied in every respect, and not for a day did she let up on her good meals. How she worked it, I am wholly unable to tell. Sometimes we would run out of a certain kind of food, and as she had about four miles to the nearest place where she could get anything, it took pretty good maneuvering to get along.

After we had the house up, nothing but a shell, as it had no plastering, we moved in sometime in April, 1865. Then we rigged up our team and our breaking plows with two four-horse teams, and with these we broke nearly the whole half-section. At the same time I hauled posts and poles from the timber, which was about four miles [away], and fenced one quarter. My brother-in-law and the hired man did most of the breaking, and I kept busy hauling wood and building the fence. We also planted broomcorn in the sod. We did all this work during the months of May and June. About this time we sold sixty acres of our land to the hired man, and this was to be taken out of Gus's quarter.

One day several years later this hired man came to me and said he wanted to sell his land. He had offered to sell it to Gus, but he didn't want it. At the time we were bargaining, I was standing on one side of the fence grinding a sickle, and he was on the other side of the fence, and before we had finished I bought his land, the team, and everything he had on the place, and he then started to go. I called him back and asked him for the terms and he said any time would do all right as he had no immediate need of the money and he would let me know in time when he did need any. I was right glad that I took it up, for at any other time I could not have bought the land so cheaply.

About this time our son, Eddie, who was then seven years old received some injury to his neck while playing at the neighbors', and these injuries proved fatal, and he died about a week later. This was a terrible blow to all of us, as he was an exceptionally bright boy and a great future seemed in store for him. His death occasioned me to sell all of my stock and implements, rent my farm, and go to Iowa. This was in the fall of 1868.

Mother and Julia and I went into Iowa in the spring of 1869. We left Charley with his Grandpa and Grandma Anderson. While in Iowa I bought about eighty head of oxen and steers. I bought from farmers in different neighborhoods with the agreement that they should let my cattle run with theirs during the summer. When I came out to gather up the cattle in the late fall, I had a bigger job than I had bargained for. The cattle had taken to the timber and the Des Moines River bottoms and it was a very hard task to break a steer out of the herd he had been going with all summer.

Finally, I got them bunched up and into a pasture, but that night I was very much afraid that they would break out and get into the cornfields. I couldn't sleep for thinking of this. After we had been in bed for a while, I heard a rapping at the outside door and as I was so tired and sleepy I didn't get up right away, but the thought instantly came to my mind that the steers had broken out. After a minute or so the same rapping came again and I then called out, "Who is there." The answer was, "Come up." I got up and my brother-in-law, August, got up too, and we went out at the same time. We walked all over the pasture and found the cattle quiet and could not see any place where they had broken through.

There was nothing more said about this incident until we reached Boone, and after I had branded the cattle there, I went to the hotel. In a conversation I mentioned the occurrence to John Linderholm, and he jumped up and said: "Good God man! I wouldn't have answered that call unless I had been well prepared with a revolver."

That was the first scare I received in regard to the matter, for it was not until then that I realized what might have happened. There was a jailbird in the woods near where we had been stopping, and, since I carried quite a sum of money while buying cattle, I had been warned against him. I believe now this was he, and if I had gone out alone I would probably have been knocked over.

This ends the story of my life, and I have tried to relate it as it happened year by year. But there are some incidents of my latter life which, I believe, will be of interest to record. However, I will say in this connection that the next spring [1870] found us again farming on the old place and I kept on farming there until 1881.

# 8

## A Solid Citizen,

## 1869–1887

I n this interval I concluded to tile the farm, as some parts of it were low and we were often obliged to wait until late before we started to work it. There was a slough running through my land from west to east and most of the time there was running water in it. I found that by tiling I would run the water off without getting any of its benefit for my cattle.[1] So I went to work trying to determine a plan whereby I could get the water up from the slough into my stockyards. I finally hit upon a contrivance which I thought would do the work for me, and I had a neighbor make it according to my plans. Well, upon experimenting, I found my apparatus would not work.

In the meantime, I had been looking over a hydraulic ram and decided I could use that in case of the failure of my own invention. So I put the ram in after an idea of my own, and to make a long story short, it worked first-rate.[2] People from far and near would come to look at it, and they thought it was the greatest thing they had ever seen in the way of hydraulics. I remember one day there were several men there, and they represented three of the surroundings counties, so you can see how widely the news of my experiment had spread. One of my neighbors, a man by the name of Crane, used to come and sit and watch the ram for hours at a time. He had a large farm nearby and a great number of cattle, so I never questioned the honesty of his purpose.

One day, during this summer, I went up to Cambridge, the county seat, and arrived home at about one o'clock in the afternoon. While I was unhitching the team at the barn my daughter Julia came running out and said,

"Come in as quickly as you can."

"What's the matter?" I asked.

"Crane has been up to Washington and is going to get a patent on your invention. Mother just read it in the *Chronicle*."

"Oh, that must be a mistake," I replied, "Crane wouldn't do anything like that."

"Well," she said, "you come in and see."

When I did read the article I found that Crane had been up to Washington, and on a certain date a patent would be issued to him. Well, I sat down for my lunch, and while eating, a neighbor of mine, Clint Thomilson, came in and asked if we had read the *Chronicle*. I told him we had, and he then asked me what I was going to do about it. I said I didn't know what I could do, but I was certainly willing to do all in my power to beat him or anyone else from getting the patent. In a short time another neighbor came in with the same question, and I gave him the same answer. Both men agreed I had better consult with a lawyer at once, but that I must be sure I had a good one.

One of the men told me to go down to Davenport, and at once my thoughts went to John Deere, the plow man, who lived in Moline.[3] I was slightly acquainted with him and knew he had had considerable experience along lines of patent fighting. The next morning I went to Moline and called on Mr. Deere. After telling him the circumstances of the case, he said there was nothing he could do but to recommend a good lawyer and one who had done a great deal of work for him. His name was Richards, and he lived in Galesburg, Illinois.

I then went home, unhitched my team, hitched up a fresh one, and after getting my brother-in-law, August Anderson, to go with me, I started for Galesburg that same evening. Galesburg was thirty or thirty-five miles distant, and we found Richards just as he was eating breakfast. After I had told him about my troubles, he said, "Well, you haven't much time to lose, and it will be nip and tuck to get the remonstrance in in time."

I told him I had been driving all night for that very reason.[4] After he had finished his meal, we went to the office of a notary and my affidavit was taken. At the same time I had an improvement on a corn planter which I considered a good thing, and so I had a drawing made of it and sent it up at the same time. Well, the long and short of it was that I got the patent on the corn planter and the water improvement, but I had to go through an interference suit with Crane before I succeeded, and that cost me a considerable amount of money.

The next winter we had our suit, and after we had been examined, Crane's lawyer wanted to compromise as Crane did not have a single witness he could put on the stand. Well, after talking the matter over with Mr. Richards, my lawyer, I decided it would be cheaper for me to accept his compromise, so I told him I would let him have the sale of the patent outside of Illinois and I would reserve that state for myself, and he finally acceded to that proposition. Although I got the patent I never made much out of it, for I put in but a very few of the rams.

In the fall of 1880, I was up at Cambridge consulting with a lawyer, Mr. Hand, of the firm of Mock and Hand, about some land the railroad company wished to buy from me, and after we had finished talking business, Mr. Hand asked me how it would suit me to run for county treasurer. I told him he might just as well ask me how it would suit me to try and run for president of the United States. I had no qualifications for the office, and whenever possible, I had always steered shy of any political activities. I told Mr. Hand I had always made it a point to keep away from the party caucuses for fear I would be put in as chairman. Hand said that was the reason they wanted me, and as he was then chairman of the county Republican committee, I told him I would think the matter over.

In the latter part of the winter I was again in Cambridge to see Mr. Hand and he again reminded me of the treasurership. I said I had spoken to my wife about it, and as she had given me no encouragement on the matter, I had just about let it drop, but I told him I would determine the matter definitely in a few days and let him know.

When I was leaving Hand's office, I met Charley Linquist, the tax collector and quite a prominent man in the county. I talked with him about the proposition, and he said it would be a good policy for me to go on a scouting trip around the county and see how things looked for my possible candidacy.

The first man I visited on this trip was the supervisor of Lyon Township, a man well liked and influential. When I finished talking with him, he came up to the buggy and said I was just the man he wanted to see run for the office. That encouraged me not a little, and I went from there to Woodhull and Galva, and everywhere I was received cordially and was very much impressed by the bright outlook. We arrived home after what appeared to me to be a very successful trip, and from that time on I decided to make the run for the position.

Mr. Holmes, who then held the office, was going to run again. I knew there was a Swede running for county clerk and that the Swedes could not expect to get two of the county offices, so I found there was some work to be done before the county convention. Well, I felt that I, as I had had no experience in that kind of work and being somewhat backward, couldn't be of much assistance in securing my election. But my friends went to work in good earnest, especially Lawyer Hand. Things developed a little slowly for some weeks.

As we were living in Cambridge at this time, I called on Hand quite frequently to keep my eye on proceedings. One day I went in there and Hand turned to me and said: "By Gosh! Hoflund, you've got to go to work. You can't expect to sit around and wear out the seat of your breeches while we are working our heads off for you."

The result was I had to go to work. I asked him which he would rather have me do—drive out among the people and tear down what he had built up, or sit around at home and do nothing. Well, he said I had to get busy anyway.

After this talk I felt I would have to try something, hit or miss. In one way I felt independent because I was fixed so that I had no need to get the office for the sake of earning my bread and butter. Well, I couldn't ignore Hand's admonition, so I set out, though I cannot describe with what reluctance I went forth.

I set out for Woodhull and in going through Oxford Township I stopped at the house of a man by the name of Cox, who was supervisor of the township. I reached [there] just as they had finished their dinner. When I told Mr. Cox what my errand was, he said he couldn't do anything for me as he had promised to support Holmes in this campaign. Well, I told him he was supporting a good man and that I had supported Holmes for the last eighteen years, and would likely be doing so at the present time were it not for the existing circumstances. Cox asked me whether or not I had had my dinner, and I told him I had not and I did not have any desire for food as I was not in a very good condition. He told his hired man to put my horses in the barn and told me to come in and get dinner. After dinner we went out and talked over the political affairs of the county, and when the hired man had hitched up my team and had driven up to the house, Mr. Cox reached out his hand and said I could count on him for any support. I told him that was really more than I expected, and you can imagine how it pleased me. That was a great deal of encouragement for me.

I arrived at Woodhull about sundown and it was raining a little. I drove up to the hotel, had my horses put in a barn, and then I went to a store. The merchant was a stranger to me, but I had been told to go and see him. He told me if I would stay around for a while the men in the wagon shops, who had gone to supper, would come in as soon as they had finished eating. When they did come, Myrtengren, the merchant, told these mechanics about my candidacy and he then told me that Mr. Osborne from Andover had just been there and he made a speech in which he said that Charles Hoflund had been pushed out by the party as a candidate for county treasurer, and he also said that the Swedes shouldn't expect to get both the county clerk's and the county treasurer's offices. He also said that Hoflund would have no show as he had no education, was not qualified for the office, and besides was well fixed and didn't need the office.

When Myrtengren told this, I got worked up a little bit and said that I didn't deny either of the statements, that I had no education, and that I had managed by dint of hard labor to bring myself to the point where I could support myself. I said further that if the people of Woodhull would lay that up as a fault against me, I had worked hard and felt as though I could support myself. I told them if they wanted to vote for Mr. Osborne because he had been in a place where he could not help but receive an education, for his father was the founder of the church in Andover and president of the Lutheran Theological College, and then if he was required to go around the county and ask the people to help him get a position whereby he could make a living and had to plead an inability to support himself, they could do so.[5]

Well, Mr. Myrtengren struck his fist on the counter and said: "By Jingoes, that's the way to talk. I have had some experience with these things, and I have found that if there is anyone who had forged ahead a little bit, there is always someone to take hold of his coattail and try and hold him back."

I cannot remember now all that was said, but the outcome of the convention was that Woodhull showed up with a full delegation for C. J. Hoflund.

I stayed at Woodhull overnight, and the next morning I drove to Galva. I went to see Thomas Milcrist, our county attorney. I expected he would spend a little time with me in canvassing Galva, but instead of that I found that he was going to Kewanee to take a postmortem testimony and had to leave as soon as he could get ready. He said I would have to go along.

Well, I remonstrated with him, but he insisted that I should go, and so I concluded to accompany him. But I did dread that trip, for I had no acquaintance there whatsoever. I did have a slight acquaintance with a man by the name of Pierce, who was supervisor. Accordingly, I told Milcrist I would make for Mr. Pierce the first thing. He went with me to his place of business, but instead of having a little time with Mr. Pierce, I found Thomas Knowers there from Annawan. He was the candidate for state legislature. He was looking up the fences in Kewanee. Pierce and Knowers went out together.

Not knowing a single person, I went out with Mr. Milcrist, and he took me to one of the banks, and I went into the private office and had quite a nice talk with the president. Farming was the topic of our conversation. From there I went to Paxton's factory, thinking I might run across someone I knew, or someone who might take an interest in my cause, but there were none of the leading men there at the time. After spending some time there looking things over, I strolled around until time for the train for Galva.

On the way to the depot I again met Milcrist, and he seemed to be acquainted with everyone he met, and before we reached the depot, we had quite a crowd following us. I was introduced to the whole bunch and made a little speech. I don't remember what I did say. After we again reached Galva, I told Mr. Milcrist that I was sorry I had gone to Kewanee.

"Why, what in the dickens is the matter with you?" he asked.

"Oh," I said, "I felt as though I have been destroying what you other men have built up."

"No you have not. Do you remember that little crowd we had before we reached the depot? Well, there was two or three of them who were Holmes' men, but after your talk they said they were going to vote for you."

I told him whether it was so or not, it was certainly a relief to hear him say that. I stayed at Galva that night, and on the way home I stopped at Bishop Hill, and also at the home of a man by the name of John Piatte.

I had been admonished by Mr. Mock and Mr. Hand that I should not allow myself to be interviewed by Captain Eric Johnson of Orion. He was editing a paper with Osborne in Moline but he lived in Orion.[6] One day I happened to be in Orion, and I got to thinking it was mighty queer I could not go up and see Eric Johnson. In thinking it over I finally made up my mind to risk a visit with him, and I finally went over to his house. Of course, Johnson knew that Osborne was candidate for county clerk and so he was hampered when it came to doing anything for me. I had a long talk with Johnson, however, and when the next paper came out I was a little curious to know what it contained. He had written a long article and in it had given me a big boost.

When the day before the convention arrived the leading men of the county met at Mock and Hand's office. The meeting lasted all night, and by morning they had everything cut and dried, although I didn't know anything about it. But I met a particular friend of mine from Geneseo, and after I had had a talk with him he expressed his opinion that I didn't have a ghost of a show. He was a delegate, but, of course, elected by the Holmes' crowd. Well, I left him and started for the courthouse and on my way I met John Hand, and as we passed he patted me on the shoulder and said everything was all right and that I could rest easy. That was all that I needed.

I went up to the courthouse and the first man that I met was Osborne, the candidate for county clerk. He was all wrought up and was swearing a blue streak. I think he must have had the news from Woodhull that the delegation was against him and was for me. From the courthouse I went home and then back just before the convention convened. When I got in I met Mr. Holmes and I took him to one side into a private room and had a friendly talk with him, and told him the situation as near as I knew it. I told him I would very likely be nominated for the office, and if he knew what was best for him, he would take things amicably and make it appear as though everything suited him all right, and by doing that he would lay up something for his future good. I told him if he didn't do that he would suffer for it. In the convention I was nominated two to one, and I, naturally, felt pretty good.

Sometime during the next July, after I returned from a trip to Eureka Springs, Arkansas, I was prompted by my friends to take my team and drive out and look over the political fences. We had a very exciting campaign. I heard some old settlers say it was the most exciting campaign for county offices they had ever seen. Mr. Holmes had jumped over the traces into the Democratic party, and had been nominated by them and he had quite a large following of disgruntled Republicans. But the outcome of it all was that I was elected by a good safe majority.[7]

I assumed the office that fall and had a good helper, so I got along all right. I would have felt a good deal better at times if I had had a little more preparation, but this didn't concern anybody but myself. The man whom I employed to assist me was Mr. S. W. Neely, and he was well qualified to fill the position. After my term had expired, he was elected treasurer. I had this man for two years, and the last two years my daughter Julia was my assistant, and she proved to be an exceptionally good one.

When my time was up in the office, I decided to go into the banking business out west somewhere. In the spring of 1887 I decided to make a trip of exploration to look up a location.

In the meantime, a man by the name of Erickson, a young man who had been in the bank of Galva for some years, came over to Cambridge to see me, for he said that he had heard I was going west to locate a bank, and he said he was affected about the same way, and he would like to make the trip with me.

We started out in the spring and went down into Kansas. We went to Wichita, which was then just over her great boom. From there we went to McPherson.[8] I stayed a few days, and, although I couldn't see any opening, I liked the place real well. We went to Arkansas City and here Erickson and I parted, and as I didn't see any place that held any inducement for me, I made up my mind to go north again.

I stopped at Holdrege, Nebraska, and from there I went on through to Norfolk. I heard they were building a railroad from there to Dodge City. While waiting for a train at Norfolk I entered into a conversation with a railroad man, who happened to be the foreman of a construction train on this branch, and he advised me to go along with him on that new road.

There were several new places, he said, and the country was a good one. I made up my mind to stop off at Scribner and go out on the branch as far as they had gone.

Between Beemer and West Point I turned to a man sitting beside me and asked him what the next stop was, and he said it was West Point. I wanted to know if there were many Swedes around West Point, and he said there were quite a few and that the county treasurer there was a Swede, and he lived on a farm between West Point and Oakland.[9] It so happened that I had heard of this Peterson, so I asked him if it was the one who was called "Post-Office" Peterson, and he said it was.

I stopped off at West Point, therefore, instead of going to Scribner, and went up to the courthouse. I had to wait some time for Peterson was busy. When I did meet him I told him what I was out for, and he said he believed he had a place for me up at Beemer, and he said he would hitch up and drive me over. We arrived about suppertime.

Peterson, who was well acquainted with the leading man of the place, received an invitation to take supper with him and this we did. This man, whose name was Beemer, said he wanted a man to start in the banking business there, and if I didn't want to come he would have to get someone else. After we had talked the matter over as well as we could, I decided to locate there, and thus my deviating journey was ended.

# Notes

## Introduction

1. Some American descendants of the Hoflund family now spell their name Hofflund or Hoffland.

2. Charles J. Hoflund, "From Djursdala to Andover, Illinois, in 1850," *Swedish Pioneer Historical Quarterly*, 22 (1971), 34–44. Beginning in 1982, the *Swedish Pioneer Historical Quarterly* (hereafter abbreviated *SPHQ*) changed its name to the *Swedish-American Historical Quarterly* (hereafter abbreviated *SAHQ*).

3. Carl Johan Hoflund, *Självbiografi*, trans. Bertil Karlsson (Vimmerby: Bertil Karlsson, 1986).

4. For the overall history of the Swedish emigration and the Swedes in America, the following may be recommended: Florence E. Janson, *The Background of Swedish Immigration, 1840–1930* (Chicago: Univ. of Chicago Press, 1931); Harald Runblom and Hans Norman, eds., *From Sweden to America: A History of the Migration* (Minneapolis: Univ. of Minnesota Press, 1976); and Lars Ljungmark, *Swedish Exodus*, trans. Kermit B. Westerberg (Carbondale: Southern Illinois Univ. Press, 1979).

5. Peter Cassel's letter of 9 February 1846, in H. Arnold Barton, *Letters from the Promised Land: Swedes in America, 1840–1914* (Minneapolis: Univ. of Minnesota Press, 1975), 32.

6. See H. Arnold Barton, "The Life and Times of Swedish-America," *SAHQ*, 35 (1984), 282–96.

7. David L. Hoffland, *Hoflund: The History of a Swedish-American Family from 1655 to 1970* (San Diego: privately published, 1971), 135.

8. H. Arnold Barton, *The Search for Ancestors: A Swedish-American Family Saga* (Carbondale: Southern Illinois Univ. Press, 1979).

## 1. The Old Country, 1834–1850

1. Djursdala Parish is located in northern Kalmar *län* (county) in the province of Småland, about 12 km. or 7.5 English miles north of Vimmerby.

2. Niclas Gudmundsson Hoflund, the first to adopt the family surname, was born in Djursdala in 1766 and died there in 1846. Cf. Hoffland, *Hoflund,* 57–59. This privately published account provides basic information on members of the family. By "whiskey," H. refers here and elsewhere to *brännvin,* a liquor similar to vodka distilled from grain or potatoes.

3. The distance from Hillebo, a croft (*torp*) in Södra Vi Parish, which adjoins Djursdala Parish, to Pelarne Church is about 20 km. or 12.5 English miles. The excursion described here was surely connected with the great "Awakening" (*Väckelsen*) of evangelical pietism that swept through much of Sweden, and notably Småland, in the middle decades of the nineteenth century. See esp. George M. Stephenson, *The Religious Aspects of Swedish Immigration* (Minneapolis: Univ. of Minnesota Press, 1932), chs. 1–3.

4. Pastor Per August Ahlberg (1823–87) was one of the most celebrated evangelists of the Swedish "Awakening." He later established a school for lay evangelists at Ahlsborg, near Vetlanda, in 1861, where many of the Swedish-American clergy received their early training before emigrating. Cf. Stephenson, *Religious Aspects,* 37–38; Yngve Bredin, "Ahlsborg and America: The Influence of a Missionary School," *SAHQ,* 36 (1985), 159–67.

5. "Djursdala" here refers to Djursdala village (*by*) in Djursdala Parish. The hamlet of Orremåla lies some 5 km. or 2.5 English

miles southeast of Djursdala village, also in Djursdala Parish. When H. says that Frödinge, a neighboring parish lay 10 miles away, he meant English, rather than Swedish miles, which are six times as long.

6. It is unclear whether Gustaf Peter Hoflund was a *torpare* or an *arrendator*. While both leased or rented farmland, a *torpare* held a croft (*torp*), part of a larger farm, for which he usually (although not always) performed stipulated amounts of labor for his landlord, whereas an *arrendator* normally leased an entire farm. Thus the title of *arrendator* generally signified higher social standing than *torpare*. The distinction was not, however, always clear-cut, for a *torp*, especially in more forested regions like Småland, could often be quite large and self-sufficient. G. P. Hoflund was in any event a man of some substance and standing in his parish. He belonged to a land-holding family and H. makes no mention of his having any tenant labor obligations. In his contract for passage from Gothenburg to New York, dated 21 June 1850, he called himself *hemmansegare* or landowning farmer. (The document is reproduced in Hoflund, *Självbiografi*, trans. Bertil Karlsson, 33). This was probably true in the sense that he had inherited his share in his father's property when the latter died in 1846, for which he presumably accepted a cash settlement from his co-heirs, which in turn would have helped make it possible for him and his family to emigrate to America. His passport calls him simply a farmer (*brukare*), without reference to property-holding. See Nils William Olsson, *Swedish Passenger Arrivals in New York, 1820–1850* (Chicago: Swedish Pioneer Historical Society, 1967; hereafter abbreviated *SPANY*), 229.

7. The hemlock, a conifer of the *tsuga* species, is native to parts of North America and Asia. H. was surely speaking here of the Swedish fir.

8. Numerous outbuildings for different purposes were characteristic of traditional Swedish and other Scandinavian farmsteads. See, for example, Sigurd Erixon, *Svenska kulturgränser och kulturprovinser* (Stockholm: Lantbruksförbundets Tidskrifts AB, 1945). Note also H.'s description of the farmsteads in Djursdala village, pages 13–15, below.

9. H.'s mother presumably learned the Methodist hymns after

the family became Methodist in America, around the time of H.'s marriage in 1860. See below, page 87.

10. Djursdala Church, built in 1692, is regarded as an outstanding example of seventeenth-century Swedish church construction and is renowned for its peasant-baroque mural paintings of Biblical scenes. The characteristic separate belfry (*klockstapel*) was built in 1698. See Dag Ljungqvist and Jan-Ingvar Andersson, *Djursdala kyrka. Vägledning utgiven av Södra Vi-Djursdala kyrkliga samfällighet* (n.p., 1979).

11. Djursdala village remains today one of the relatively few Swedish clustered villages of the older type to survive the widespread land reallocations (*jordskiften*) of the nineteenth century. It thus looks today much as H. here describes it. Djursdala Parish as a whole was relatively little affected by the reallocations, and its landholdings remain still largely fragmented and intermixed. During the seventeenth century, taxable land was divided into *mantal* (or *hemman*) of varying size for fiscal purposes. Cf. Barton, *Search for Ancestors*, 22, 67–68; also Eli P. Heckscher, *An Economic History of Sweden* (Cambridge, Mass.: Harvard Univ. Press, 1954,), 127n., 155–66.

12. Home distillation of *brännvin* was a profitable sideline to farming, as it converted perishable surplus grain and potatoes to an easily stored, transported, and salable product. Until 1855, the amount of legal distillation was based on the size of the farm. From that year, it was limited to home consumption until that, too, was prohibited in 1860, due to widespread misuse of alcohol and the growing influence of the termperance movement, largely associated with the religious revival.

13. The old craft guilds (*skrån*), of medieval origin, retained much of their monopoly over the skilled trades in Swedish towns and cities until their special privileges were abolished in 1846. Some have nonetheless survived to the present day as trade associations that set standards for training and quality.

14. Although the Swedish parliament, or *Riksdag*, first passed a law requiring a school in every parish in 1842, literacy was already remarkably widespread in Sweden by that time. Cf. C. Emanuel Carlson, "The Best Americanizers," in J. Iverne Dowie and Ernest M. Espelie, eds., *The Swedish Immigrant Community*

*in Transition: Essays in Honor of Dr. Conrad Bergendoff* (Rock Island, Ill.: Augustana Historical Society, 1963), 31–50. Carlo M. Cipolla, in his *Literacy and Development in the West* (Harmondsworth: Penguin Books, 1969), 72, 115, estimated adult literacy in Sweden in 1850 at fully 90 percent, the highest rate among the major European countries in his tabulation for that period and slightly higher than that of the adult white population of the United States at that time. Djursdala's first permanent schoolhouse was not built until 1872. (Barton, *Search for Ancestors*, 71.).

15. The earliest emigrants to America from Södra Vi and Djursdala parishes went to the Andover area in Henry County, Illinois. Samuel Jönsson, who left Södra Vi in 1846, settled there the following year. There were no further emigrants from Södra Vi until 1849, when forty-three persons emigrated from the parish, mainly to the Andover area in Illinois, as well as the first emigrants from Djursdala, who went generally to the same place. Thereafter, Södra Vi, Djursdala, and surrounding parishes were among the earliest in Sweden to contribute large numbers of emigrants, most of whom settled initially in northwestern Illinois. See Olsson, *SPANY*, passim, esp. 77, 165; Barton, *Search for Ancestors*, 44–45, 75–76.

16. Regarding the "America-letters" and their significance in encouraging increasing emigration, see Barton, *Letters from the Promised Land*; for some further, characteristically enthusiastic descriptions of America by early Swedish emigrants in the 1840s and 1850s, see George M. Stephenson, "When America Was the Land of Canaan," *Minnesota History*, 10 (1929), 237–60.

## 2. The Journey to America, 1850

1. Berg, located where the Göta Canal leaves the western end of Lake Roxen, some 12 km. or 7.5 miles north of Linköping, was around 100 km. or 62 miles north of Djursdala. The Göta Canal, connecting the Baltic with the North Sea via Lakes Roxen, Vättern, and Vänern, was completed in 1832. Before the construction of the railway trunk lines in the 1860s, many of the

early emigrants from south-central Sweden traveled via the Göta Canal to Gothenburg, taking their last departure from accompanying friends and family at the locks at Berg.

2. Motala, where the Göta Canal enters Lake Vättern from the east, grew up with the construction of the canal and its mechanical workshop, or factory, established in 1822 to produce necessary machinery for the canal. *Wrede* (or *vrede* in modern spelling) means "wrath" or "fury."

3. The falls at Trollhättan, where the Göta River runs out of the southwestern end of Lake Vänern and the canal descends via numerous locks, remains a celebrated tourist attraction. This westernmost section of the waterway, the Trollhättan Canal, was completed in 1800. H. surely meant here that he had no recollection of anything between *Trollhättan* (not Motala) and Gothenburg.

4. Gothenburg (Göteborg), Sweden's second-largest city (after Stockholm) and leading seaport, was the main port of embarkation for Swedish emigrants throughout the entire period of the great migration.

5. During the eighteenth century, Sweden had become one of the world's leading producers of iron. When exports to Great Britain languished during the early nineteenth century due to rising British competition, Sweden developed a lively iron export to the United States, from around the 1830s down to the outbreak of the Civil War in 1861. During that period, most of the early Swedish emigrants traveled directly to America on Swedish sailing vessels, usually as extra cargo on top of a load of bar iron, as in the case of the Hoflund family and their fellow passengers aboard the *Virginia*.

6. The members of the Hoflund family who took passage to America aboard the *Virginia* were: the farmer (*brukare*) Gustaf Peter Hoflund (1806–86), his wife, Anna Brita Carlsdotter (1810–91); and their children Carl Johan (1834–1914), the author of these reminiscences; Carolina (1837–56); Maria Lovisa (1839–1931); Johanna Sofia (1840–91); Gertrud Lotta (1852–99); and Alexander (1847–1911). Two other children were born to the family in Illinois: Josephine (1851–1934) and Gustaf Frederick (1854–1935). G. P. Hoflund's sister Stina (1803–64), her husband, Lars Magnus Jonsson

(c. 1803–50), and their children, Carolina Josephina (1839–64) and Albert Joakim (1847–1904) accompanied the Hoflunds, but L. M. Jonsson died in Gothenburg before embarking, as here described. (Olsson, *SPANY*, 228–31; supplemental information from Hoffland, *Hoflund*.).

7. Olof Wijk (not Olaf Wyke), the elder (1789–1856), was a prominent Gothenburg shipowner and exporter in the iron trade. In 1829 he had visited the United States on business, where he kept an interesting travel diary, given in Per Clemensson, ed., *Två göteborgare på resa i Nya och Gamla Werlden* (Göteborg: Landsarkivet i Göteborg, 1978). An English translation is forthcoming. Note that in this contract, G. P. Hoflund styles himself as "landholder" (*hemmansegare*). (See Ch. 1, n. 6.)

8. The bark *Virgina* had previously carried emigrants from Gothenburg to New York in 1846, 1848, and 1849. (Olsson, *SPANY*, 72, 152, 180.) In 1848 it took some emigrants to New Orleans. See Nils William Olsson, *Swedish Passenger Arrivals in U.S. Ports, 1820–1850 (except New York)* (St. Paul: North Central Publishing Co., 1979), 61–62.

9. The passenger list for the *Virginia*, upon its arrival in New York on 3 September 1850, shows that it carried 74 passengers, one of whom died at sea. (Olsson, *SPANY*, 228–31.)

10. The United States Census of 1850 showed a total of 3,559 Swedish-born persons in the country at that time. See Axel Friman, "Swedish Emigration to North America, 1820–1850," *SPHQ*, 27 (1976), 153–77, esp. 153 (for the census figure). Friman provides a detailed statistical analysis.

11. John Ericsson (1803–89), famous as the inventor of the screw propeller in 1843, had come to New York in 1839. His construction of the Union ironclad *Monitor*, which in 1862 defeated the Confederate *Merrimac* at Hampton Roads during the Civil War, made him a popular hero and the most prominent Swedish American of his day to the general American public.

12. Olof G. Hedström (1803–77), a former seaman who had gone ashore in New York in 1825, became a Methodist missionary and between 1845 and 1875 he had a floating chapel, the Bethel Ship *John Wesley,* where he preached to and helped thousands of arriving Swedish and other Scandinavian immigrants. In addition

to being the real founder of Methodism in his native Sweden, Olof
Hedström in New York and his brother Jonas in Victoria, Illinois,
(to be encountered later) laid the foundations for Methodism
among many of the early Swedish immigrants in America,
including eventually the Hoflund family. See Stephenson,
*Religious Aspects*, esp. 117–19; also Henry C. Whyman, "Peter
Bergner, Pioneer Missionary to Swedish Seamen and Immigrants,"
*SPHQ*, 30 (1979), 103–16.

13. Before the railroad network reached Chicago in 1852, most
passengers and freight traveled from the East Coast to the Midwest
over the route followed here by the Hoflunds: by steamboat up the
Hudson River from New York to Albany, via the Erie Canal
(completed in 1825) to Buffalo, and from there by steamboat to
Great Lakes ports.

14. Swedes had been settling in Chicago since 1838, and by 1850
it was becoming what it would thereafter remain, the leading
Swedish-American urban center. By the end of the century, it was
considered the world's second-largest "Swedish" city, surpassed
only by Stockholm. See Ulf Beijbom, *Swedes in Chicago: A
Demographic and Social Study of the 1846–1880 Immigration*
(Uppsala: Läromedelsförlagen, 1971). Lars Magnus Spaak (Speake)
from Djursdala Parish arrived in New York with his family aboard
the *Virginia* in August 1849. They moved from Chicago to
Princeton, Illinois, in 1851. (Olsson, *SPANY*, 180–82.)

15. The United States Census for 1850 showed a population for
Chicago of 29,963.

16. The Illinois and Michigan Canal was opened in 1838,
connecting Lake Michigan at Chicago with the Illinois River at La
Salle, Illinois, below which the river was navigable down to the
Mississippi at Grafton. Cholera was endemic in the years around
1850. For another Swedish account of travel over this same route
and the ravages of cholera in 1850, see Barton, *Letters from the
Promised Land*, 57–59.

17. This Steinholm (or Stenholm) had evidently been a fellow
passenger on the *Virginia*. (Olsson, *SPANY*, 228.) To have brought
over something as large and heavy as a farm wagon from home was
unusual, but note that even the Hoflunds brought a small cart
with them. (See page 40, below.) Regarding material possessions

that the Swedish emigrants took to America, see H. Arnold Barton, "Måns Jakob's Grindstone, or Documentary Sources and the Transference of Swedish Material Culture to North America," *SAHQ*, 38 (1987), 29–40.

18. The self-proclaimed prophet, Eric Jansson (not Johnson) (1808–50) was leader of a perfectionist sect in Sweden in the early 1840s. Persecuted for apostasy from the Lutheran state church, he went to America in 1846 and established his own sectarian community at Bishop Hill in Henry County, Illinois, to which there came some 1,200 of his followers, chiefly from the provinces of Uppland, Västmanland, and Hälsingland, over the next several years. In May 1850 Jansson was shot to death at the county courthouse at Cambridge by John Root, a Swedish-born adventurer who had married a woman in the colony whom Janson had prevented from leaving there. After continuing to flourish through the early 1850s, the colony disbanded in 1860, although the community, with many of the old colony buildings still exists. See esp. Paul Elmen, *Wheat Flour Messiah: Eric Jansson of Bishop Hill* (Carbondale: Southern Illinois Univ. Press, 1976), and Olov Isaksson and Sören Hallgren, *Bishop Hill: A Utopia on the Prairie* (Stockholm: LTs förlag, 1969).

19. The next sizable Swedish settlement in Illinois, after Bishop Hill, was Andover, also in Henry County. The area was acquired and a town platted by a New York-based colonization company in 1835 and a few settlers, mainly New Englanders, came out over the next few years, including a lone Swede in 1840. More Swedes arrived in 1847, and henceforward Swedish settlement proceeded apace. In 1849, Lars Paul Esbjörn (1808–70), the first ordained Swedish Lutheran pastor to serve his countrymen in the American Midwest, established himself at Andover, and in 1850 the community's first Lutheran church, called the Jenny Lind Chapel after the celebrated Swedish soprano who contributed generously to it, was built. From Andover, Swedish settlement spread to other, nearby localities. By the 1860s the now-overcrowded Swedish settlements in northwestern Illinois were sending forth numerous "daughter" colonies to the advancing frontier to the west and north, to states like Iowa, Nebraska, and Minnesota. Thus Andover, with a present population of less than 200, retains a

particular prominence in the annals of Swedish settlement in the Middle West. See esp. Ernst W. Olson, Anders Schön, and Martin J. Engberg, *History of the Swedes of Illinois*, 2 vols. (Chicago: Engberg-Holmberg Publishing Co., 1908; reprint ed., New York; Arno Press, 1979), 1: 272–97; Helge Nelson, *The Swedes and the Swedish Settlements in North America*, 2 vols. (Lund: C. W. K. Gleerup, 1943; reprint ed., New York: Arno Press, 1979), 1: 165–66. Cf. also *The History of Henry County, Illinois* (Chicago: H. F. Kett & Co., 1877), 524–28.

20. Anna Lovisa Zachrisdotter came in 1849 from Sweden to Andover, where her husband and children died of cholera. Here she married a German, Otto Lobeck, and eventually moved to Nebraska. (Olsson, *SPANY*, 167.) Their son, Charles Otto Lobeck (1852–1920), served as a Democratic congressman from Nebraska from 1911 to 1919. See *Biographical Directory of the United States Congress, 1774–1971* (Washington, D.C.: United States Government Printing Office, 1971), 1300.

## 3. Early Days on the Illinois Prairie, 1850–1851

1. Jonas J. Hedström (1813–59) came to America in 1833 and settled by 1838 at Victoria, Knox County, Illinois, where he became a blacksmith and Methodist missionary, and established the first Swedish Methodist church in America in 1846. By the later 1840s, his elder brother, Olof Hedström of the Bethel Ship Methodist mission in New York, referred growing numbers of arriving Swedish immigrants to Jonas in Illinois, which played a major role in the early concentration of Swedish settlement in Henry, Knox, and adjoining counties. (Cf. ch. 2, n. 12, above.) See esp. Olson et al., *History of the Swedes of Illinois*, 1: 176–82.

2. In 1849 Eric Jansson purchased a large tract of land in this part of western Henry County for the Bishop Hill colony, which lost it through default in 1851. Thereafter other Swedish settlers moved in. The town of Orion was founded in 1853. See Olson et al., *History of the Swedes of Illinois*, 1:312–13.

3. Rock Island had its beginning with Fort Armstrong, established in 1816, and was incorporated as a city in 1841. The

Bishop Hill colony set up a fishing camp there in 1848 and thereafter Swedes settled in the community in growing numbers. By the end of the century Rock Island, together with neighboring Moline, was among the largest urban Swedish-American communities in the United States, with Augustana College, which moved to Rock Island from Paxton, Illinois, in 1875, as a leading cultural center for Swedish-American Lutherans. See Olson et al., *History of the Swedes of Illinois*, 1: 291–94; Nelson, *Swedes and Swedish Settlements*, 1: 169–71.

## 4. The Great North Woods, 1851–1852

1. Wisconsin became a state in 1848, by which time there was considerable settlement in its southeastern corner. By 1851, when H. came to work in the Eau Claire area, this western part of Wisconsin was still largely a wilderness. Although there had been an Indian trading post at Eau Claire in the later eighteenth century, the community began to develop in the 1850s, in connection with the logging of the "pineries," and was only incorporated as a city in 1872. Cf. Robert C. Nisbit, *Wisconsin: A History* (Madison: Univ. of Wisconsin Press, 1973). Regarding Swedes in the region, see Emeroy Johnson, "Swedes in Northwestern Wisconsin," *SAHQ*, 38 (1987), 1–12.

2. Gage's problem in paying his men's wages may have been caused, at least in part, by the 1848 Wisconsin state constitution's prohibition against the establishment of banks, resulting in a great shortage of credit, which was only repealed by a referendum in 1852. See Nisbit, *Wisconsin*, 219–20, 223, 233–34.

3. It is not clear what H. meant here by a "shamrock" swamp. Chances are he was confusing "shamrock" with "hemlock."

4. Stillwater lay some 11 miles south of the present Scandia in Washington County, near the site in 1850 of the first Swedish settlement in Minnesota, which in time would be known as the most "Swedish" state in America. Just inland from Taylors Falls, some 30 miles up the St. Croix River from Stillwater, lay what would become the important Swedish settlement around Chisago Lake, in Chisago County, first settled in 1851 and made famous

through the Swedish novelist Vilhelm Moberg's fictional depiction of Swedish peioneering life there in his novels *Unto a Good Land* (1954) and *The Last Letter Home* (1961), published by Simon and Schuster in New York, as well as through Jan Troell's films, *The Emigrants* and *The Good Land*, based upon them. See Ernst Skarstedt, *Svensk-amerikanska folket i helg och söcken* (Stockholm: Björck & Börjesson, 1917), 44–45; Emeroy Johnson, "Early History of Chisago Lake Reexamined," *SAHQ*, 39 (1988), 215–25.

5. Jonas Westerlund arrived in America with his family from the province of Hälsingland in Sweden in November 1850, settling in Andover, Illinois. His younger brother, Peter Westerlund, later became one of the leading citizens of Orion, Illinois. (Olsson, *SPANY*, 252–53; Olson et al., *History of the Swedes of Illinois*, 1: 313.)

## 5. Making Ends Meet, 1852–1855

1. The directory for Western Township, Henry County, for 1877 shows "Just. Hofflund" (Gust. Peter Hoflund) as the owner of 80 acres in Section 35, valued at $5,000, and notes that he was "one of the first of his country people to come to this town." (*History of Henry County*, 377.) The same source shows Charles Samuelson, born 1827 in Sweden, immigrated to America 1851, and arrived in Henry County 1852, as the proprietor of 350 acres, worth $19,200. (Ibid., 382.) Gustaf Peter Hoflund died in 1886; his wife, Anna Brita, in 1901. (Cf. ch. 2, n. 6, above.)

2. "Ague" was the common term to describe the fits of chills and fever caused by malaria, which was widespread at that time in both Europe and America.

3. Altona, in Henry County, was largely settled by Swedes. Among the earliest were the brothers P. Petterson and G. A. Erickson from Djursdala, who arrived in Altona in 1850 and quickly became the community's leading business entrepreneurs. See Olson et al., *History of the Swedes of Illinois*, 1: 321–24; also Barton, *Search for Ancestors*, 82.

4. Here H. obviously means that he learned to read *English*,

since he could read Swedish before he came to America. (See page 21, above.)

5. Commodore Cornelius Vanderbilt (1794–1877), the New York shipping and railroad tycoon, was considered a byword for wealth and power during the Gilded Age.

6. The Chicago & Rock Island Railroad was completed in 1854, only two years after Chicago received its first rail connection with the East Coast. In 1856 the first railroad bridge across the Mississippi was opened at Rock Island, allowing the rapid spread of rail communications in the West.

## 6. Loggers, Indians, and Tight Money, 1855–1856

1. A number of Indian tribes, mainly of the Algonkian-language family, inhabited Wisconsin. Those H. encountered were very likely of the Chippewa (Ojibwa) tribe.

2. From what H. relates here, it is not clear whether Mechum had hoodwinked Manning, or vice versa.

3. This Stone, who is not previously mentioned, had apparently undertaken to collect for H. his unpaid wages for his first logging job at Eau Claire in the winter of 1851–52, under the promissory note from Gage, H.'s employer there. (See page 49, above.)

## 7. Settling Down, 1856–1869

1. Swedona, in Mercer County, Illinois, was largely settled by Swedes, mostly from Östergötland and Småland, beginning in 1849. See Olson et al., *History of the Swedes of Illinois*, 1: 320–21.

2. On Methodism among the Swedish Americans, see esp. Stephenson, *Religious Aspects*, 256–263. It may be wondered whether, in fact, the "Mr. Fletcher" H. here referred to was not the Swiss-born English theologian John William Fletcher (originally de la Fléchière) (1729–85), John Wesley's revered collaborator, whose writings continued to be reprinted during the nineteenth century.

3. Christine Anderson was born in Bottnaryd, Jönköping *län*

(county), Sweden, in 1842 and came with her family to America in 1852. (Hoffland, *Hoflund*, 88.)

4. The directory for Osco Township, Henry County, for 1877 lists Charles J. Hoflund, a Republican and Methodist born in Sweden, as the owner of 294 acres. (*History of Henry County*, 471.)

5. The children of Charles John and Christine Hoflund were: Edmund (1861-68), Julia (1864-1957), Charles Elwood (1867-1944), Almeda Christine (1870-1962), and Oliver (1873-1958). Hoffland, *Hoflund*, 88, 130-44, gives details on their lives.

## 8. A Solid Citizen, 1869-1887

1. "Tiling" here means laying down covered tile pipes to drain the soil, an increasingly common practice during this period. Cf. Barton, *Search for Ancestors*, 115.

2. A "ram," in this sense, is a hydraulically operated water pump.

3. John Deere (1804-86), a pioneer blacksmith from Vermont, perfected a steel plow that went into production in 1843 at Grand Detour, Illinois. In 1847 he moved to Moline, Illinois, where he founded the firm incorporated in 1868 as John Deere & Co., today one of the world's largest manufacturers of agricultural machinery and for generations a major employer of the large Swedish-American population of the Rock Island-Moline area.

4. From Orion to Moline to Galesburg, H. had driven around 55 miles that day.

5. Joseph E. Osborn (originally Esbjörn) was born in Hille, Gävleborg *län*, Sweden, in 1843. He was the son of Lars Paul Esbjörn, the first ordained Swedish Lutheran pastor in the American Midwest, who came to Andover, Illinois, in 1849, and who served as the first president of the Swedish-Norwegian Augustana College and Seminary in 1860-63, before returning to Sweden. (See ch. 2, n. 19, above.) Joseph Osborn, who remained in America, served in the Union Army during the Civil War and was later a journalist, businessman, civil servant, musician, and 1871-73 agent for an American railroad in Gothenburg, Sweden. See

Olsson, *SPANY,* 189; Olson et al., *History of the Swedes of Illinois,* 1:682–84.

6. Eric Johnson (1838–1919), born in Österunda, Västmanland, Sweden, was the eldest son of Eric Jansson, leader of the Bishop Hill colony. He was a captain in the Union Army during the Civil War and thereafter followed a peripatetic career as editor of both Swedish- and English-language newspapers, merchant, land speculator, and civil servant. Together with the journalist C. F. Peterson, he was author of the first history of the Swedes in Illinois, *Svenskarne i Illinois* (Chicago: W. Williamson, 1880), one of the very earliest works of Swedish-American historiography. Cf. Olson et al., *History of the Swedes of Illinois,* 1: 795–96; Ernst Skarstedt, *Pennfäktare* (Stockholm: Åhlén & Åkerlund, 1930), 90–91.

7. Since the election of Abraham Lincoln in 1860, the great majority of Swedish Americans had been traditionally Republican.

8. McPherson, the seat of McPherson County, Kansas, lies at the southern edge of a sizable area of Swedish settlement in McPherson and Saline counties, centering on Lindsborg, developed by the First Swedish Agricultural Company in Chicago and the Galesburg Colonization Company, organized in the later 1860s by land-hungry Swedes in Illinois. See for example Emeroy K. Lindquist, *Smoky Valley People* (Lindsborg, Kans.: Bethany College, 1953); Nelson, *Swedes and Swedish Settlements,* 1:271–81.

9. Cuming County, in northeast Nebraska, where West Point and Beemer are located, adjoins Burt County to the east, where the area around Oakland was heavily settled by Swedes. See Nelson, *Swedes and Swedish Settlements,* 1: 290–91.

# Index

H. Arnold Barton is Professor of History, Southern Illinois University at Carbondale, and Editor of the *Swedish-American Historical Quarterly.* He is the author of numerous books and articles on the Swedish-American experience, and is himself descended from immigrants from Djursdala, Charles J. Hoflund's old home parish in Sweden.